D1450979

PASTORAL WORK

AND

PERSONAL COUNSELING

Books by Russell L. Dicks

———

THE ART OF MINISTERING TO THE SICK
Co-author with Richard C. Cabot M.D.

MEDITATIONS FOR THE SICK

WHEN YOU CALL ON THE SICK

AND YE VISITED ME

YOUR SELF AND HEALTH

WHO IS MY PATIENT?

THE MINISTRY OF LISTENING
(A PAMPHLET)

PASTORAL WORK AND PERSONAL COUNSELING

Pastoral Work

and

Personal Counseling

RUSSELL L. DICKS

NEW YORK

THE MACMILLAN COMPANY

1945

Second Printing

PRINTED IN THE UNITED STATES OF AMERICA
BY THE VAIL-BALLOU PRESS, INC., BINGHAMTON, N. Y.

TO DALE AND BILLY

TWO LITTLE BOYS

who brighten our lives in dull moments,
humble our spirits in proud moments,
and
warm our hearts in tender moments.

PREFACE

WHEN *The Art of Ministering to the Sick* was published in 1936 the Right Reverend Henry Knox Sherrill, Bishop of the Episcopal Diocese of Massachusetts wrote, "This is the first modern book that describes the pastoral task." At that time I was conscious of the fact that we had written of but two of the many responsibilities the minister faces as a pastor, namely, ministry to the sick and to the bereaved. Since that time I have determined to describe the whole of the pastoral task and have consistently collected material for the past several years for that purpose.

The war has increased the need for an examination of the pastoral field, particularly that of personal counseling. The military chaplain tells us that seventy-five per cent of his work, as a conservative estimate, is in work with individuals. The result of this experience is that literally thousands of men and women will turn to the clergyman for personal counseling in the immediate years ahead. Unless the clergyman can be of help in the capacity of counselor this great opportunity for the church will be lost.

Our clergy are poorly prepared for the task of pastor and personal counselor. In our training we are where the medical profession was at the time of the introduction of the internship for the training of physicians. The theological seminaries belatedly are stirring themselves to the task of more adequately training their students to meet this vital ministry. It will be another ten years before anything approaching adequate programs of pastoral training can be established. Even then the pastors already serving churches will not be benefited. *It is for the purpose of assisting the average clergy-man serving the average church to take advantage of the opportunity and meet the responsibility of the pastoral task before him that this book is written.*

RUSSELL L. DICKS

Chicago
July, 1944

CONTENTS

ix

PART ONE

PASTORAL WORK

CHAPTER I

PASTORAL WORK

PASTORAL work is as old as religion but it takes on new meaning in the light of modern psychology and with the coming of increased stresses of living. These stresses are brought about not only by the war but by our becoming an urban nation where we are forced to live intimately with our neighbors.

Psychiatry, as a specialty in medicine, became popular during World War I through its study and treatment of the so-called shell shock victim, although the foundations of psychiatry had been laid before the war. The psychoneurosis, as a personality condition, has been popularized for the general public in World War II. It is too early to anticipate what organizations or persons will carry on the bulk of treatment for these thousands of persons dismissed by the military as psychoneurotics, who have come to believe they are different from their fellow creatures. However, one result is certain and that is that *personal counseling* as a method for helping individuals who feel emotionally insecure is becoming popular.

During the past twenty years some of our clergy have become increasingly interested in the subject of pastoral work and personal counseling because of the light modern psychology is throwing upon human behavior. While this light has been considerable still most investigation in the field of human personality and behavior remains to be done. Personal counseling stands more naturally in the tradition of the clergyman than it does in any other profession, but even so we have made little contribution to the subject in recent years; in fact we have been shouldered almost out of our own field by physicians and social workers.

Although some of our clergy have carried on certain types of pastoral work consistently in the past we cannot say that we have worked diligently nor even with intelligence at the task. During the past fifty years the Protestant clergy have become more and more interested in ideas and less and less interested in people as individuals; the result is that the art of pastoral work and personal counseling has been lost. Our clergy have run hither and yon, promoting this and that but have come increasingly to overlook the spiritual needs of the individual parishioner. Overhead committees, boards, and programs have occupied so much of the minister's time and energy that it has become practically impossible for him to carry on pastoral work.

We permitted this situation to develop because we were afraid actually of coming to grips with the problems of individual persons since we have not been trained to understand them. We have waited for further light; with the coming of light we have been slow to accept it. The result has not been flattering. Young people's problems have seemed too involved, old people's problems uninteresting, sick people's problems were left to the physician, while the problems of unmarried people seemed fraught with danger. The result has been that our clergy have baptized the babies with pious words, married the young with little counsel, buried the dead with little hope and stood helplessly before the bereaved. It is safe to say that eighty-five to ninety per cent of the clergy today are doing little effective pastoral work or personal counseling of any kind.

Now we are slowly awakening to our task but many of our ministers still struggle against the awakening. Modern psychology strikes a responsive note in the minds of some who are willing to settle down to hard work and study, and to subject the results of their work to examination. All too often this field has been left to the sentimentalists who neither knew nor admitted they ever failed. We recognize that God limits Himself to the limitations of those who serve Him.

The clergyman's task in pastoral work is to assist spiritual forces at work within the individual; forces which are struggling for growth and maturity of the soul. These forces follow laws which are as dependable as are the laws of health within the physical body. In fact, we are recognizing that the spiritual and physical affect each other so profoundly that many observers claim they are but different parts of the same whole.

Life is a growing process, a maturing experience, a stabilizing force,—never finished, never complete. The purpose of living is to develop spiritually mature human beings; maturity to the place of accepting and carrying through responsibility in the creative process of the universe of which we are a part; maturity to the place that we may feel comfortable without forcing our wills upon others; maturity to the place that we are willing to let others be free thus gaining freedom for ourselves. We gain maturity of soul so that we may come into fellowship with God which is to gain eternity, or the immortal life.

As a parent I love my child. I cannot explain why, there are a dozen, a thousand reasons. He may tear my heart through his suffering, but as a wise parent I know he must be permitted to live his life, to find his way to school, to defend himself against the neighborhood bully. I also know he faces the possibility of becoming the neighborhood bully unless as a father I am wise enough to avoid bullying his mother, brother and himself. What a hard job it must be to be God!

It is the pastor's task to assist that maturing, growing, developing life in his parishioners and those who seek his help. Some will need a great deal for a little while; others will need it for a long time; some will need a little for a little while; others will need none at all. It is the pastor's task to discover the need and to attempt to meet it. Throughout his work he must be alert lest he make the mistake God does not make: he must not live someone else's life.

As clergymen we are not content with relieving suffering as the physician and social worker are. To be sure we are concerned that suffering shall be relieved; witness the church's building of hospitals and colleges for the care of the sick and the relief of ignorance, that the abundance of nature may be tapped for mankind; but with all this we are not content. It is not enough to be free from want and to have health. As clergymen we are concerned with what you do with health when you have it. It is the pastor's task to work to relieve suffering and fear and loneliness, but it is also his task to assist people to gain faith and hope and that fellowship with God which encompasses eternity itself. This may be accomplished even though suffering is not relieved. It is accomplished sometimes not only in spite of suffering but because of suffering. One of the most spiritually mature people I have met is a woman who has never walked a step in her life.

As we think of ourselves as God's assistants let us be certain of our point of view. There is much of mystery in religion for there is much in the Mind of God we do not understand which will always be true since our perspective is limited. Three times, twice in calm moments and a third in a heated moment of suffering, our Lord seemed to portray the mind of God more clearly than at any other time. Once He told the story of a Samaritan, whom He described as "good," who picked up a stricken man beside the road. Our Lord did not speak of the spiritual care of the man upon the Jericho road but we assume that it was implied in the story in the phrase, "he had compassion upon him." Another time our Lord clearly revealed God's Mind in His story of the Prodigal Son. The son was returning home, asking only that he be permitted to work in his father's fields. To his amazement, and to ours today whenever it happens to us, for this is one of the great mysteries of religion, *the father was out upon the road to welcome his son's return*. There was no thought in the father's mind of the son's going to the fields. The point of the story is the father's attitude toward his boy's shame.

Finally, upon the cross our Lord demonstrated the mind of God in turning that tragic experience into one of triumph. The cross was tragic and we must never overlook that fact. There was suffering there over and above the suffering of our Lord. Mary, His mother, was there, and Mary Magdalene, who loved Him deeply, His disciples, His followers and friends, and all those who looked for a new day for the poor, dispirited and discouraged. There was tragedy in the blind prejudice of those who misunderstood Him and caused Him to be put to death. There was tragedy in the pitiable weakness of Pilate and in the blind brute-strength of the soldiers who raised the cross with Him upon it. There was tragedy in our Lord's suffering, but beyond the suffering there was the peace, the quiet strength, the hope that His mastery of the cross revealed. There we see the deeper Mind of God.

These three scenes the pastor must have burned into his soul as he sets out upon his task: the giving of physical relief to the man upon the Jericho road, the father out upon the road to welcome the returning son, and finally, the triumphant living that may come out of suffering and tragedy, even out of death itself. In the light of these revelations the pastor goes to his task with a quiet confidence that God is about His work in the universe and that they who make understanding a part of wisdom are privileged to assist Him.

CHAPTER II

THE PASTORAL TASK

THE French physician, Fondeau, described the doctor's task in these words, "To cure sometimes, to relieve often, to comfort always." This ideal might well be used to describe the clergyman's pastoral task.

"*To cure sometimes.*" There are a certain number of spiritual crises, difficulties, emotional blocks, problems, which can be relieved; which must be relieved if the person suffering is to take up his task again and know spiritual happiness. To give relief to a patient, who without treatment would have died, is a rare experience for a physician. So in the spiritual area such opportunities are rare for the clergyman. Occasionally through our efforts a person is helped spiritually who would not have been helped otherwise; not often but "sometimes."

Richard Cabot used to say, "About once every five years, if you are alert and lucky, you will have a chance really to do something significant to help someone." One of those rare opportunities he used to cite came to him through the request of a friend who was dying who asked that he play his violin for her. He cancelled all other engagements, came to her home and there quietly in another room where she could hear the soothing strains of music, he played selection after selection, as she slipped away. Richard Cabot was an able violinist; not many of us have talents that would enable us to take advantage of such an opportunity as that but others come to us.

Such a rare chance came to me while I was serving at the Massachusetts General Hospital in Boston. A four-year-old child, whose parents lived in New Hampshire, was dying. They requested that the child be baptized which was done. In the days that followed I kept in touch with the progress of the youngster. On Christmas Eve word came to me that she was not expected to live through the night. I spent most of the night with the parents as we watched the slow struggle that dying often becomes. Early the next morning the child died. I went with the mother and father to the hospital office, then took them in my car to the station where they would catch a train home. At the station, which was hot and over-crowded, we found that another train would not leave for New Hampshire until late afternoon. I knew that the mother would be in the hospital herself before six hours had passed if she waited there. After some difficulty I persuaded them to permit me to drive them home in my car. While it took most of the day I have never known a Christmas in which I felt I more nearly served the Lord than I did that day.

Not all our opportunities involve such unusual circumstances; but they almost always involve suffering on someone's part. A sailor came into the Y. M. C. A.—U. S. O. in Norman, Oklahoma, and began to curse the State Dry Law. The U. S. O. director heard him and eased his way over to the sailor's side. Presently he said, "How have you been getting along?" The sailor replied, "I've been trying to get leave so I could go home and do a job of killing. I've just had word from my wife that she is going off with a soldier." The director said, "Come back in my office where we can talk it over." There he got the story. The sailor and his wife had lived together seven years although they had never been married; they had a child five years old. He had just heard from her that she loved another man; he felt he wanted to kill both of them; since he could not get leave he was trying to make up his mind whether to "go over the hill" or not. They talked for an hour, at the end of which time the sailor got up and thanked the director, saying he felt a lot better but he still did not know what he was going to do. The director invited him to come and see him again. A week later he was back. He said, "I've decided I'm the lucky one after all. If she wants that guy she can have him."

We do not know whether or not that talk prevented the man from going home and killing his wife. Certainly we may be sure it made him feel better because it gave him a chance to relieve his feelings.

"To relieve sometimes." To help a person gain relief from suffering is easier and more common than effecting a cure or bringing about a major change of attitude such as our fathers in the faith thought of in the conversion experience, which becomes less and less frequent as our attitude toward religion changes. As pastors we ought to be able to aid in bringing that relief fairly often even though we do not change the objective problem. Often we deal not with the problem itself but with the parishioner's attitude toward his problem, himself, his fellows, his God.

A soldier came into his chaplain's office and said, "Chaplain, I've got trouble. There's nothing I can do about it and there's nothing you can do about it, but I want you to let me get it off my chest." He talked for twenty-five minutes while the chaplain listened. At the end of that time the soldier got up and said, "Thank you, chaplain. I feel better." There was no doubt in the chaplain's mind but that the soldier did feel better.

The relief of suffering is one of the pastor's functions, for unless relief is gained our parishioners cannot go on but break down under the strain whether the suffering is physical or spiritual. As pastors, however, our concern is with the spiritual for others work with the physical; sometimes we do combine our efforts with the physician, the social worker and the economist to bring about relief, but often we work alone for there is no one with whom we may join forces.

One day in a Southern city where I had been speaking an attractive girl of twenty-six or seven waited until the others had gone. She quickly introduced herself, then added, "I'm desperate. If I don't get some help I'll kill myself. I know I will. I just can't go on the way things are going." She spoke rapidly, her face was flushed, her voice tense, and tears came to her eyes. I said, "Whom have you talked to?" She said, "I've talked to no one. I can't talk to anyone I know. I've known my minister since I was a little girl, he used to hold me on his knee. He wouldn't understand, and I can't afford to go to a doctor." I said, "Tell me what seems to be the trouble." She said, "I love my mother very much. She's a dear to us, but we have had to live with her because my husband does not think I ought to work and he doesn't make enough for us to afford our own home. My mother completely dominates us. I can't even discipline my own child. We have no privacy. When my husband and I quarrel we have to do it in a whisper. I do love my mother but she just does not understand." So the story went. Her husband felt he was unable to afford the kind of a house she deserved and to give her the servants she needed. She was willing to do her own work and live in a hovel if need be. It was obvious she did not want to cut her own throat but she would not have minded taking a few slices at her mother's, while I felt her husband's pride was what needed a little trimming. However, that was not the first task.

We talked for perhaps twenty minutes and at the end of that time I said, "Come back to our class tomorrow and we will talk again when it is finished." The next day she said, "I slept last night for the first time in weeks." During the week we had five brief conferences and I arranged for her to see a physician after I left her city if she needed to. I also urged that she write me when she wanted to, which she did regularly. Each time when I answered I would ask, "When are you going to move?" After nearly two years her husband bought a house (he could not bring himself to rent one), and she was happy for the first time in years. That did not solve all their problems; deep problems are not solved that easily. But it did bring some relief.

Months later when we were talking again, I said, "Do you think you would have committed suicide if we had not talked?" She said, "I am sure I would have. Also I never would have stuck to my determination to move if you had wavered in your single point, 'When are you going to move?' "

A chaplain, serving on board a transport during the early months of the war, told me of a pastoral task not many of us would welcome. His ship had stopped at a port in Australia to pick up refugees who had been evacuated from Java by air transports. A Dutch girl came on board with her husband. When she saw the chaplain's insignia she said, "I must talk to you." The chaplain arranged to see her the following day. During the next few days he saw the girl and her husband for five conferences. The girl did most of the talking although her husband followed her conversation closely and emotionally shared in the whole experience.

The girl and her husband, a Dutch government official, along with their three children, had been evacuated by air from Java. Their plane landed at an Australian port early in the morning; before a boat could reach them from shore the Japs came over and straffed the plane. The girl's husband, who was forward in the plane was wounded; she ran to him just as an explosion threw the two of them free of the plane, but the children were burned to death. The husband had been badly burned and for a time it appeared as if he would not recover, but he had gradually fought his way back. The accident had occurred three months before but either they had not sought a clergyman or had been unable to talk about their experience until they came on board the transport where they met the chaplain.

I questioned the chaplain closely as to the conferences he had with the couple. The first three had been given almost entirely to the girl's relating the story of the accident and to her talking about their home, as well as her early home life and religious beliefs. Her question was, how could they continue their lives when they could not seem to recover from the shock of the loss of their children; neither could she seem to reconcile their loss with God's Benevolent Love.

The chaplain wisely let her talk, asking questions and encouraging her with his interest but he did not attempt to answer her questions until the fourth conference. Each time he said, "We will talk again tomorrow." By the fourth conference she seemed to be more relaxed and said that she had been sleeping better. He then explained to her that the loss of her children was a great one but that so far as the children were concerned he believed they were all right. This, he reminded her, was the Christian doctrine as found in our Lord's teaching in the New Testament concerning little children. Finally, he pointed out that she was young and that she might have another family.

When the couple left the ship in New York City the girl told the chaplain, "You will never know how much you have helped us." A few months later he heard that they had adopted a refugee child and that the girl was again pregnant.

"*To comfort always.*" One day a twelve-year-old youngster was going to the operating room to have tissue cut from around his heart. Even when we are twelve we know that this is serious. Eagerly he looked up at me, "Do you think it'll be all right?" he asked. "Sure it'll be all right!" I said, as confidently as I could. I didn't know whether the operation would be successful or not but I believed he would be all right even though he might not recover.

A woman who was dying told me with difficulty, due to her extreme illness, "I wish I had lived a better life." That seemed to me as clear an effort to make a confession as anyone ever expressed. I said, "You have lived a good life. You have nothing to worry about." She smiled and closed her eyes for my prayer.

Another said, "You will come and be with my sister when I go, won't you? I don't want her to be alone."

Two student nurses came to me for counsel within a week, both with the same problem. They were Protestant girls engaged to marry Roman Catholic boys and both boys were insistent that the girls come into the Roman Catholic Church. One girl had started her instruction, then had broken it off because of the priest's negative attitude toward her former church. When her future mother-in-law heard the girl had stopped instruction she said she would not come to the wedding if it was held in the rectory. In our counseling conference we discussed the girl's attitude toward the church, her future mother-in-law, her fiancé, and her fiancé's attitude toward his mother, in an effort to discover how much he was going to permit his mother to dominate him and his wife. I asked her to bring him to me for a further talk, which she did. As we talked I felt his attitude toward the girl was healthy and that he had a good deal of understanding of his mother; while he was intolerant of his fiancée's church he was willing to have her return to it if she were unhappy in his. Basically they were in love. Further the girl's understanding of God was greater than any church; the church in her thinking was a means to an end, not an end in itself. I asked if she would like to continue her instruction; she said that she would. She followed my suggestion that she go to another priest and talk her problem over with him, and she has now resumed her instruction.

This was not a satisfactory solution to her problem. There was no reason for her leaving her own church which she loved. Her future mother-in-law was intolerant and probably will cause her considerable trouble, and her fiancé was unreasonable. Nevertheless they had fallen in love and their plans for the wedding and their future were made. She wanted to join the church of her husband to avoid having a divided home. I encouraged her to do so.

The other girl's problem was the same but her attitude was very different. She said, "I will not give up my church for anyone. We will be married in the Presbyterian church or we will not be married. We always quarrel about religion." The boy was ten years older than she was; she was only nineteen; he had been away for two years but was coming home soon and was insisting that they be married. I said, "How much do you love him?" She said, "I don't know. I've almost forgotten what he looks like." I said, "How hard will it be to break off your engagement?" She said, "Not hard for me. I've already written him how I feel about our differences of religion and that ought to do it. But I just wanted to talk it over with someone." I said, "I think you did right. You have no chance of making a success of your marriage with your differences of opinion upon religion and I think a priest would tell you the same thing."

We comfort in many ways, largely by our own attitudes. There are many who desire this attention and care—"benefit of clergy" they call it—and no one else will do. This is particularly true in time of sorrow. People are willing to be married by a civil authority, to raise their children without sending them to church but when a member of the family dies they want to see a clergyman. "You have words of authority at such a time," a young physician once told me.

There are other times than in bereavement when we may comfort those who are afraid, discouraged, lonely. When we approach our task properly we may comfort even those who but stand and wait.

If there are those who say this description of the pastoral task falls short of bringing individuals to Christ I would say this is of the essence of Christ; this is living religion. Presently we will examine methods where we will see that point more clearly.

To cure sometimes, to relieve often, to comfort always. We are not always sure what is a *cure* and what is *relief* and what is *comfort* in pastoral work. Sometimes they overlap. We cannot be as certain as can the physician in his work, but even he is not always certain. The doctor follows the principle: "Wait and see." If the symptoms do not recur then it is a cure, if they return after a time it is relief, if they persist but the patient is helped to endure them it is comfort. So we test our results in pastoral work as the physician tests his: wait and see.

In the medieval Irish Catholic literature there is the statement, "It is to be hoped that every person will have a soul-companion." That is the pastor's task. To be a soul-companion to those who need such companionship. It is walking along the way with a friend; sometimes the distance is short, with only the need or opportunity for a word, a smile, a hand clasp. Sometimes it is a longer way. In sickness and in pain, in birth and death and bereavement, in pain and fear and loneliness, in greed and selfishness and lust, the son is returning home. "Neither do I condemn thee."

CHAPTER III

THE PASTORAL CALL

WE HAVE been accustomed to speak of all our pastoral work as *visiting*. This is unfortunate and illustrates how naïve we have been in our conception of the pastoral task. Visiting is characterized by "You tell one and I'll tell one"; it is a mutual exchange of pleasantries. Too much of our pastoral work has been just that, a mutual exchange of goodwill. We recognize that goodwill is the foundation upon which pastoral work builds and at the time the term *visiting* came into usage by the church fathers it probably carried a different connotation than it carries now.

Due to the lack of training and discipline in the preparation of our clergy for pastoral work and because our people have not been instructed in what to expect by way of pastoral ministration, we have often not even known what pastoral work is or when we were doing it. One pastor I know sets himself the goal of one hundred pastoral calls a month. If he rings a door bell and no one answers, he leaves a card calling that a pastoral call, and rightly so. When he calls following a death and sees the whole family that is counted one call. If he has lunch with two men he counts that two calls because he has been in touch with two families. Another minister I know does not count a conversation he may have on the street corner with a parishioner regardless of the content of the conversation, yet if he calls upon the same parishioner in his office he counts it a pastoral call. If a parishioner comes to his office for five minutes it is a pastoral conference; yet a thirty-minute telephone conversation, regardless of the subject discussed, is not counted. Another clergyman I know regards as a pastoral contact every person he greets during the whole day. I have wondered whether he considers kissing his wife good morning a pastoral contact. His records would indicate that he does.

The military chaplains have faced this problem of what to count as a pastoral contact for they have had to list their personal conferences in their official reports to Washington. Their figures have run amazingly high but then their opportunities have been great. "In six days since coming to this post," said a Navy chaplain, "I have done more real pastoral counseling than I did in six months as a civilian pastor." Likewise an Army chaplain said, "In six months I have had more opportunity to help individual men than I had in ten years as a minister in civilian life."

"It is not uncommon," said a Service Command chaplain, "for our chaplains to have as many as twelve interviews after supper." I sat with a chaplain as he was interviewing men in the guardhouse. These were new men who had been admitted during the past twenty-four hours so that this was the chaplain's first contact with them; this was the time when he was to make or break his ministry with them. He saw twenty-three men in an hour and fifteen minutes. He had held as many as eighty such interviews in a day, he explained.

One afternoon I sat with a Navy chaplain as he interviewed men who were awaiting orders to move to various parts of the country, many of them going directly to the fleet for active combat duty. Every man was greeted with a colorless, "Sit down, friend, what can I do for you?" The requests were varied but the answer was to the point. One boy came to inquire how he could find out about a buddie whose neck had been broken and who was in a civilian hospital. With him the chaplain took more time; he commended the sailor for his interest in his friend and presently asked him if he had a New Testament. The boy brightened, said that he did have and thanked the chaplain for his offer. The chaplain said he would inquire about the boy's injured friend and asked him to come back the next day. There was no offer to call the hospital then and inquire if the injured man could be seen by his friend and to help him secure shore leave that evening.

Another afternoon I made calls with a Navy hospital chaplain who went from bed to bed seeing some hundred men in two hours. Each man he greeted in exactly the same way, "How are you, fellow?" He explained that he covered the whole hospital of five hundred beds, every day. In that way when the men wanted to talk more or had some request to make they could easily speak to him. One man did stop him to ask if the chaplain could help him get a transfer to a hospital nearer home.

One chaplain explained, "Our problem is to get rid of the men, push them on. It is not a question of having interviews. It is a question of getting through." Another said, "Sometimes we have to out-talk a man rather than listen to him. Otherwise we would never get through." A much more wholesome attitude was expressed by a chaplain who said, "I run about eight to twelve office interviews a day. I can handle that many but I wouldn't like many more." That is about what the most effective pastor can handle: when he goes over that number he cuts down his efficiency.

A civilian minister I know regularly reports from two hundred to two-hundred-fifty calls a month. When I told him that was too many he agreed but said that when he calls upon a parishioner in the hospital he always sees fifteen or twenty other patients who are non-parishioners.

An elderly clergyman used to call in our Boston hospital

quite early each morning. His coming was a joke among the patients and nurses. He went from ward to ward, walking through each one, not stopping to speak to anyone but just saying, "Good morning," as he passed along or often only nodding. He had been coming to the hospital for years, yet even the nurses who had been there five years or longer did not know his name. When a patient wanted to see a clergyman no one ever thought of the old gentleman, yet a conscientious church board was paying his salary and he was reporting "a great work" in the hospitals of Boston with the "poor, unfortunate sick and dying."

There are several conditions which can be used to identify a pastoral call or conference. The place where the conference takes place is not one of them. The first condition is *time*. No one can say how long a call should take, regardless of the type of call it is. A physician reviewed one of my books in which I had said five minutes may be too long for one call in the sickroom while an hour may be too short for another. The physician took violent exception to the latter part of the statement. "Never," he said upon his authority as a physician, "should a call in the sickroom last over fifteen minutes." On many occasions, particularly in acute illness, the doctor is right. But one cannot say, "Never," one can only say, "Hardly ever!"

I was a patient in a convalescent hospital where our greatest burden was time. The hospital was several miles from New York City where my friends lived. If anyone came to see me, as a few did, and stayed less than a full hour I was offended. More harm was done than if no call had been made. You cannot make calls, even calls upon the sick, by the clock.

A famous Boston pastor is reported always to have called by

the clock; ten minutes for each call in each home. He never took off his coat, he never sat down. Never, or hardly ever, did people seek his help when they were in trouble.

In routine home calling where no stress is known to be present and where one member of the family is seen I find my calls last approximately twenty-five minutes. When there is more than one person present they run thirty to thirty-five minutes when something important is talked about; otherwise they are ten or fifteen minutes. New-member calls run thirty to thirty-five minutes; calls upon the bereaved ten to fifteen minutes; that is, the call which is made immediately upon the notice of death. The follow-up call which is made the day after the funeral may require thirty minutes or more, depending upon the emotional needs found to be present. Sick calls run from two minutes to thirty minutes. Office conferences run an hour when dealing with stress; office calls for planning a wedding or for pre-marital counseling are apt to be shorter, because I do the talking and thus save time by being more direct in dealing with the subject under discussion. This is because I am dealing with more factual material as differentiated from the emotional experience which characterizes so much office counseling. Perhaps it is more accurate to say the emotions which are present in marital counseling point in a different direction than those present in other counseling. I have had many telephone conferences where stress was present which ran as long as thirty minutes.

One clergyman told me, "I had a woman in my office recently for three hours. I couldn't get rid of her. She was leaving town three days later and would not get to see me again, so she wouldn't leave." If he had said to her at the end of an hour, "Now you're tired, and I'm tired and we will not gain anything by talking more today. I'll see you tomorrow at ten o'clock," she would have been willing to leave. Three one-hour conferences will accomplish something spread over three days, while one three-hour conference not only loses everything gained during the first hour but definitely does harm to both counselee and counselor.

The woman did not want to leave my friend's office because she needed more help. She would have been willing to leave, however, if she could have looked forward to seeing him the next day. He should not have asked her if she would like to come back. He should have told her to come back and have set a specific hour for the conference. That removes all responsibility from her mind for having to decide whether she wants to return and for trying to decide what they will talk about. She may, upon reflection, realize she has told him everything she can think of concerning her problem. It is not that he wants more information; he knows information is not the important factor in counseling but the emotional-healing experience that goes with it. When the woman returns for the second conference the pastor will decide what she shall talk about, in the light of her emotional condition at that time. In three conferences a great deal can be accomplished; in one three-hour conference a counselee will only become confused and exhausted.

The element of time in a given pastoral conference, whether the conference takes place in the parishioner's home, his hospital room, his office, the pastor's study, upon a street corner, or over the telephone is important because it takes time for two minds and two sets of emotions to come positively and creatively into play in relation to each other. This is discussed at length in chapter IX. The creative emotional experience is the healing experience. While this may start instantaneously when two persons meet, still time is needed for it to develop. The immediate response such as our Lord seemed to be able to release in persons he had never met before is rare, so rare not many of us should expect it to happen in our ministries, just as not many of us can look forward to death upon a cross.

To be sure there is sometimes an instantaneous emotional response in the sickroom. An interesting thing about illness and suffering is the way it breaks down reserve and inhibitions. Many sick persons will readily respond emotionally to interest and goodwill and may speak quite frankly of their appreciation. Sometimes this is embarrassing to the physician, nurse or pastor; it should not be. I have had patients hold my hand to their lips and kiss it after we had had a particularly helpful prayer. A friend told me of a dignified clergyman who went to call upon a woman parishioner who was quite ill. Several members of the family were in the room at the time of his call. After he had talked quietly with them for a time he had a prayer. As he rose to leave the sick woman, who was partially disoriented and who mistook the minister for a relative said, "Uncle, kiss me before you go." The clergyman crossed the room to where the sick woman was lying, bent over and kissed her upon the forehead saying, "Goodnight, my daughter, and peace be with you."

There was a man with a pastor's great heart. How often have we seen those who needed above all a pastor's arm about them and a pastor's kiss, but we are held back by our own inhibitions and by the people around us who would not understand, most of whom need the same thing but are "buttoned-up" by prejudices and frustrated feelings.

We cannot say how long a pastoral conference will take but we are not justified in counting a call that does not permit the parishioner to speak of his soul's condition. This is the "eternal you" for the pastor. In pastoral work when examining human behavior we search for the "illusive why" since all behavior is purposeful; this search is important only because of our interest in the "eternal you." Any pastoral situation that does

not permit a discussion, a confession, an expression of well being, or discouragement by the parishioner is not a pastoral
contact. This may have to do with the parishioner's physical
self, his business, his job, his home, his church, his prayer life;
that which concerns him is his soul's concern. In pastoral work
we start with the parishioner where he is in his interests, emotions and needs. Our ultimate concern, however, is not what
is happening to him but how he *feels* about it.

A pastoral conference may come to this point quickly or it
may not. Having arrived, the time that is needed to deal with
the parishioner's attitudes, his mind, his emotions, varies
greatly. In fact, work at this point is the art of pastoral care
and counseling. My point here is just that unless a clergyman
in his pastoral contacts permits the parishioner's attention to
turn to his soul's condition and takes time to deal with whatever condition is present, then a call is not a call and the pastoral
work of that minister is failing. "How are you today, fellow?"
was an honest effort to do just what I am talking about. The
failure lay in the fact that time was not taken to deal with what
was found.

There are a dozen ways of reaching the "eternal you" in
pastoral work and those ways must be varied. What we do
once we are with a parishioner is determined by what we find.
Just because stress is not always found does not mean we are not
doing sound pastoral work. Thank God, every person we call
upon or talk to does not need help; but when trouble is found
we must be prepared to deal with it.

Some clergymen who are serving large parishes say, "I do
not have time to work with people as you describe pastoral
work. I can't take thirty minutes with every person I see."
Every person you see will not need thirty minutes. This thing
of "being busy" is a defense for ignorance on the one hand and
fear, or lack of faith, upon the other. Any pastor who regularly

has four pastoral contacts a day, *as a minimum,* who works carefully and honestly, following up those contacts and does the meditation, records and prayer each calls for, will be a great and an effective pastor. There is no church so small and none so large but that every pastor who serves it should be able to have four pastoral contacts a day.

Those calls which are made where no one is at home and a card is left should be counted, just as should those times you call at the hospital and cannot see your parishioner for various reasons. They should not be counted in the same category as the calls I have described earlier in this chapter. Calls where the parishioner is not seen prepare the way for future work; they remind the parishioner that you are thinking of him and interested in him. They should be listed as Class B calls, however.

On the other hand a significant pastoral contact is not determined by stress being found to be present, by a person talking about his Christ or his God or by a parishioner asking for prayer. That is determined, to summarize, by reaching a discussion of his spiritual condition and by taking time to deal with that need. In other words, a pastoral call is determined by the method used; its *effectiveness* is determined by other conditions.

CHAPTER IV

GENERAL INSTRUCTIONS

1. Do no harm. If you can avoid doing harm you will help ninety per cent of the people with whom you work in pastoral calling and personal counseling.

2. Do not give advice. If you tell a person what to do in the major areas of living it becomes your decision and helps no one. The giving of advice is dictatorship in living. The pastor's task is to assist the parishioner to make his own decision, even though the pastor would have made a different one. The pastor may help most by reminding a person of the alternatives in a choice.

3. The pastor holds the far view. Perspective in pastoral work is essential. What happens today is important but regardless of what happens today tomorrow will come; life goes on.

4. Suffering may be creative. It is the pastor's task to help the parishioner turn suffering into creative channels. What happens to a person is not important; it is the way he feels about it that makes it creative or destructive.

5. Recognize the parishioner's emotional level and work with him there. People are at different levels in their religious development just as they are of different chronological ages. Religious development and chronological ages do not correspond.

6. Pastoral work and personal counseling are in the emotional realm more than in the intellectual. The pastor's presence, interest, faith and affection, more than his opinions, are helpful.

7. Spiritual healing of mental attitudes comes through fel-

lowship. The pastor must gain the parishioner's confidence. The person who does not like you cannot be helped. You do harm by being too persistent.

8. Time is an important factor in fellowship; it cannot be hurried, neither must it become a burden.

9. The parishioner will choose his own spiritual consultant: if he prefers a physician, a friend, a social worker, or another clergyman that is his right.

10. In pastoral work and counseling the parishioner will carry you to his need if given a chance. We talk about our own problems, interests, needs when we are with someone we like.

11. The pastor must go to the people through routine calling if they are to come to him in time of difficulty. The home is a sacred place; one call in the home is worth three in the office or place of business.

PART TWO

OPPORTUNITIES FOR PASTORAL WORK
AND PERSONAL COUNSELING

CHAPTER V

THE PASTOR GOES TO HIS PEOPLE

MANY pastors ask, "How do you get pastoral counseling started?" By pastoral counseling they only visualize people coming to them for help. Others say, "No one ever comes to me for help." The tragedy of missed opportunities is contained in these words.

Pastoral work consists more in the pastor going to the people than it does in their coming to him, for the pastor who goes to his people ultimately will find them coming to him. In our study of human personality we have considered the abnormal in order to be able to recognize and understand the normal. We are now studying the normal, the commonplace, the usual. I used to assign my theological students' calls upon persons where there was known suffering; now I assign routine calls where no stress is known to be present when the call is made. It is surprising in what a large number of these calls stress is found.

As pastors we are interested in people first and problems second. Our point of view is: your problem is of no great concern to me aside from you and what it means to you, for I am not interested in which or how many of the commandments you have broken; I *am* interested in what the breaking of them means to you. In the same way I am interested in what you are facing and what you have been through in terms of your own spiritual condition.

With this thought in mind need we ask, "What are the opportunities for pastoral work? Is it necessary to get established in a church and become acquainted before you start your pastoral work?" It is not! The need for getting acquainted and established in a new church in and of itself presents an opportunity for pastoral work. To meet the official board, the teachers of the church school and the officers of the women's society formally at a reception is one thing but to hunt them out individually in their places of work and homes is quite another; to sit down and ask questions of them about their work, their families, their length of time in the church, their interests and hobbies is the essence of pastoral work when done properly. The wise clergyman starts his pastoral work immediately upon arriving in a community to take up work in a new church.

While the pastor, of necessity, will call first upon his official board, the officers of his women's society, his church school teachers and his young people's leaders upon starting his work in a new church, I would not place these calls of first importance in pastoral work. They are necessary administrative calls which afford an opportunity for pastoral work and which lay the foundation for future work, for out of these calls will come information of special spiritual needs which may be followed up. It will not be surprising to those who know my background of hospital work that I place first in pastoral work calling upon the sick and dying. The sick and dying are followed in importance by the bereaved and special cases such as those needing relief, jobs and medical care. In war time these special needs include the families of men and women in the military service. Next in order of importance for pastoral work are: the shut-ins, new members, prospective members and finally the routine call where no stress is known to be present. While the routine call is placed last in this list effective work with those mentioned earlier turns upon the routine call, as I shall point out later. The routine call is sowing the seed, these other calls which deal with stress are a reaping of the harvest. There is no harvest where the seed is not sown.

In all these calls the pastor goes to the people. They await only his time and energy. The pastor who is established, acquainted and known to be interested in people may become so busy in office counseling and the community's affairs that he fails to find time to make routine calls. That is unfortunate. The fault lies usually in poor planning and a distorted sense of values, in permitting oneself to become involved in too many extra-church, extra-parish activities, for too many of our ministers are running around tending someone else's patch, going to meetings, making speeches. Whenever a pastor fails to make calls regularly in all of the above categories he is failing in his ministry.

A. THE SICK AND DYING

It is difficult to predict the future so far as the clergyman's work with the sick is concerned. Through an increasing emphasis upon psychosomatic medicine the physician is coming to recognize the importance of the spiritual needs of his patients both as a cause of illness and as an aid to the recovery of health. The trend is toward the physician taking over this phase of the patient's care himself, however ineffective that care may be. If this trend continues as it has in the past ten years the clergyman's work will come under close scrutiny by the doctor. At present the average physician would like to bar ninety per cent of all clergymen from the sickroom; one cannot but be sympathetic with this desire in view of the utter lack of preparation by the clergyman for this most delicate of all delicate tasks. At the same time we know more now about the task of ministering to the sick than ever before; our clergy are becoming better trained for the pastoral task; and we are looking toward a day when we may join hands with the physicians in the care of the sick.[1]

Ministry to the sick and dying calls for the greatest skill of all pastoral work. With or without this skill, however, we are still welcome in the sickroom because the need there is so great. If we can just avoid doing harm we will be able to help ninety per cent of the people we call upon who are sick. A Boston surgeon lectured to my theological students upon the subject, *What Not To Do in the Sickroom*. He went down the line with fifteen or twenty negatives: don't talk too much; don't stay too long; don't ask the patient what is wrong with him— if he wants you to know he will tell you; don't argue with the patient; don't tell him he is going to die; don't talk about someone else you know who had his disease and how long he was sick; don't force your prayer upon your patient; don't pray too long. A month later he stopped me in the hall to say, "In my lecture to the boys I overlooked the most serious mistake they will ever make in their work with the sick. I've just had two patients whose ministers made it. That is in failing to call at all upon their sick parishioners. That's one they'll never be forgiven."

Methods in ministering to the sick are the same as those used in other pastoral work and personal counseling which are discussed in later chapters, but there are certain major conditions in the sickroom in which more stress is present than in

[1] *The Art of Ministering to the Sick*, Cabot and Dicks. The Macmillan Company, New York, 1936.

Religion and Health, Hiltner, chapter 2. The Macmillan Company, New York, 1943.

Religion in Illness and Health, Wise, chapter 2. Harper & Brothers, New York, 1942.

Who Is My Patient? Dicks. The Macmillan Company, 1942. For nurses but contains significant new material for the clergyman; especially section on "Religious Needs of the Sick."

others which must be discussed here. While we should not distinguish between one parishioner and another so far as our efforts are concerned, it is certain that if our interest is in helping people and not primarily in making a good annual report, we will have to spend more time with one person than with another.

There are four situations in the sickroom which afford the clergyman his greatest pastoral opportunity. These are not exhaustive in that significant spiritual needs will arise under other conditions in illness, but in these stress-situations lies the greatest opportunity for the pastor. He should call upon as many of his people who are sick as he can but he should call more frequently and persistently upon persons going through these experiences.

1. The surgical operation is a stress-situation, a personal crisis. From the surgeon's standpoint there are major and minor operations; from the patient's standpoint all are major—some are just more serious than others. The element of uncertainty and the dread of pain are present in every surgical patient. The surgical operation is a spiritual experience, an experience of faith; faith in the surgeon, frequently an unknown person to the patient; faith in the nurses who are to care for the patient; faith in the hospital, its personnel and equipment; and faith in God working through nature to effect healing.

A Boston surgeon described the surgical operation as a religious rite. He said, "We have our high priests and acolytes, our ritual, incense and blood sacrifice." The acceptance of the religious rite by the god of surgical operations affects the patient more than any other person participating in the ritual. It is with faith that he goes into the ceremony, so he prepares himself before the operation, purging his conscience and examining his belief.

A patient in a Chicago hospital told me of having told a lie ten years before. Why did she feel the need to make this confession after ten years? Because the next morning she was facing a serious surgical operation during which she knew she might die. I had talked and prayed with her frequently but when she came seriously to prepare herself for the uncertain future, that lie stood out in bold relief against the background of the pending operation.

I used to ask pre-operative patients routinely the question, "How do you feel about it?" Ninety per cent answered, "My faith is in my surgeon and God." The surgeon was thought of before God but then he had been punching them around recently in his examination and was more real to them. Perhaps they were right anyway, in thinking first of the importance of the surgeon, for a surgeon can ruin God's efforts, while we know God will not spoil a surgeon's work.

Since the surgical operation is a religious experience, an experience of faith, a parishioner will need any help the pastor can give him. In my early work as a hospital chaplain practically all of the requests which came from patients themselves for my services were from pre-operative patients. As one girl, facing an operation for cancer of the lung, put it, "I know the surgeon can do only so much and that the patient must do the rest. I was afraid I wouldn't be able to do my part so I wanted to see a minister." She was right in her reasoning. A minister ought to be able to help her at that time. I think I did; I know I did later as she approached death.[2]

The time to see a parishioner who is facing surgical treatment is the night before the operation. There are several reasons for this choice, the primary one being that through the pastor's reassurance the patient may be helped to relax and thus secure a good night's sleep, which is needed. To be sure, most physicians give a sleeping potion but even a drug is aided in its work

[2] *The Art of Ministering to the Sick*, p. 359.

by the patient's cooperation. Another reason for calling the night before is that the pre-operative routine of the hospital is avoided. Most surgeons start their work quite early which means the patient is prepared even earlier. The result is that although the clergyman may arrive at the hospital at daybreak he invariably interrupts the pre-operative preparations.

The minister should, whenever possible, be present during the operation, sometimes going into the anaesthetic room with the patient; then returning to the family to be with them during the long wait. Some ministers like to be present to watch surgery. I have done this frequently; more experience has led me to believe the pastor's place is with the family once the patient is asleep, however.

2. The second major stress-situation we see in illness is in the person facing life with a physical handicap following his illness. Loss of eyesight, loss of hearing, loss of a limb or limbs, inability to walk through an injury to one's spine, joints stiffened by arthritis, restricted activity following a heart attack, diabetes which necessitates the regular taking of medication, the colostomy treatment for cancer of the rectum, which involves radical and disfiguring surgery; these and others are conditions calling for heightened courage and adjustment on the part of the patient.

The mental workings of a person facing life with a handicap are complicated. At that time especially he is thrown back upon his basic beliefs, his faith. To injure one's body is to injure one's soul, for an injured body means a hurt spirit and broken pride. "This has happened to me," we think, "to me of all the people I know." Then we ask the question, "*Why?* Why has my world, my God singled me out?" Most of us can find reasons for what has happened to us; even though our conclusions are actually quite unfounded. For instance, a guilt feeling is more apt to be present in a person facing life with a handicap than in a dying person. It is little comfort to point out to a handicapped person how many others have the same condition; in fact, it may do harm, unless the physician or clergyman doing so has the complete confidence and affection of the patient.

Since the facing of a handicap is a spiritual experience, as is the facing of an operation, here again is a need and an opportunity for the clergyman. Not always will a patient want to talk about this problem with his clergyman but he should be given the opportunity to if he wishes. Sometimes he will be helped most by being treated perfectly naturally by the clergyman; this is especially true if there is a feeling of guilt present. It may be weeks, months, even years before a person can talk about his attitude to his pastor and then it may be quite a different attitude from the one he had at the onset of his handicap. That is why I never push a person who is in this condition. I take plenty of time, am natural and easy, but I do give many opportunities for the patient to talk about himself if he wants to. As God's representative I am willing to face anything my parishioner wants to talk about. In that way I try to demonstrate God's affection in the face of suffering.

Above all, handicapped persons do not want a sickly, sentimental sympathy. They want to think of themselves as natural, normal, healthy people. If they are treated otherwise they withdraw and become depressed. A woman who had a tracheotomy tube in her throat told me of hearing one of a group of school children say to the others as they passed her home, "The woman who lives there has a tube in her throat!" Imagine the heightened feeling of isolation which followed!

A man of thirty-five became paralyzed as a numbness in his feet crept up his legs and into his hands. Then for some months his disease did not progress, but he was confined to his chair and bed. He reviewed his whole situation—his future, his family, his financial resources and what his handicap would mean to his attractive young wife and two children. He concluded that the insurance money would educate the children and after a time his wife would probably remarry, so he planned to commit suicide. Before he could carry out his plan the disease began to advance. Eventually he found his way to our hospital and it was there I got to know him. He was a talented musician and a brilliant conversationalist. We spent hours together talking of many things but never of his plan to commit suicide, his lost music or his inability to work. It was months later that we reached the place in our relationship where we could talk about his suicidal plan and his future.

Another person with a terrific handicap asked me quite seriously to help her plan her suicide as there was no reason for her continuing to live. All she had to do was to stop taking an expensive drug for a few days and the job would have been done but she had never thought of that and I did not feel inspired to point out anything so obvious. She never committed suicide, but I think she derived a good deal of pleasure contemplating it.

The first days when a parishioner is facing a handicap are important ones for the clergyman and he will do well to call frequently and in a leisurely way. To face a handicap is to feel alone, deserted by God and isolated from friends. The pastor can do much toward overcoming both these feelings.

3. The long convalescence is another stress-situation found in illness. For some barren spirits anything after two days is a long convalescence, while for others the crisis of time does not set in for weeks. There are a number of diseases which call for long confinement to bed, to a wheel chair, to hours where activity is limited and the sufferer is dependent upon those around him. After a while he tires of reading and his imagination runs bare, then loneliness and boredom possess his spirit like devils dragging a soul to hell. When he has passed the

physical crises and is moving slowly up the long road toward recovery the physician turns to more acute problems, the nurses are dismissed, families go about their tasks, and his friends accept the fact that he is out of the picture; they may call, but, having been once, they go on about their own affairs. Then he comes to the conclusion that no one really cares after all, and he sees that the world can go on without his help.

The clergyman's ministry is important during acute illness and he must not neglect it, but *his greatest opportunity* in ministry to the sick is with the person going through a long convalescence. His first call during the early days of an illness is taken for granted—everyone calls then; in fact too many call. His second call is hardly expected but is accepted with appreciation. "Great fellow, that minister," says the patient, "he really gets around." Boredom is beginning to set in so that when the pastor calls a third time he is greeted like a long-lost friend; the fourth and fifth and sixth calls follow and instead of "parishioner-minister" it now becomes "Fred and Joe." Family and friends are astonished at an interest and devotion to religion that seems to have started with father's illness. I repeat, the minister's greatest opportunity is with the long convalescent.

4. Those facing death present the fourth major crisis of illness. It is impossible to separate the ill from the dying or to be able to describe one's work as ministering to the sick at one point and to the dying at another. In fact, the distinction is unimportant. In general we have to admit that the Protestant clergy have let this vital ministry get away from them, with the exception of the Lutherans and Episcopalians. The free churches, the Methodist, Baptist, Presbyterian and others increasingly have moved away from a ministry to the dying.

In this ministry the clergyman reminds the parishioner of what he may forget, not by what he says but by his presence.

Prayer is his primary method. Through prayer dormant, spiritual resources are released which strengthen the parishioner. Dying is a lonely experience. Through prayer the parishioner is helped to realize he is not alone; that as he has known the companionship of God here, so he will know it more there; as he has been strengthened by loved ones here, so he will find loved ones there. Dying is a spiritual experience and the way one dies is a demonstration of faith and courage. At this point more than at any other the clergyman's own faith and quietness of spirit give strength. Especial care must be taken by the clergyman to conduct himself in a natural, friendly way. Our clergy have failed at this point frequently, so that the "funeral tone of voice" in clergymen is a description of a sentimental approach to death which all people of faith bemoan. The proper conduct in the presence of the dying is one of quiet, hopeful dignity and poise. Due deference should be paid the experience in which we are participating. Humor is out of place there as well as later in calling upon the bereaved. A clergyman once made the remark that he never had complaints from the corpses he buried. While such a remark may seem clever because it is bizarre, at the same time it reveals a barrenness of soul which is extremely regrettable in a minister. The Reverend Walter Morley of Chicago once said, "Where there is no respect for the dead there is no respect for the living."

B. THE BEREAVED

Bereavement is a personal crisis. It is characterized by loneliness. It matters not how strong one's belief in personal immortality may be, there is still the problem of separation which must be faced when a loved one dies. In bereavement the question of why a given person, particularly a child or young person, dies is raised frequently. There is seldom much question about the aged—the family say only, "We knew it would come but we were not ready."

We saw in the preceding section that the clergyman's great opportunity to be of help to the sick comes with the people who are going through a long convalescence because of the problem of loneliness. He faces another such opportunity with the bereaved. Many of the questions and thoughts which arise in the minds of the bereaved have to do with things which are beyond the common mind, that is, they deal with God's justice, God's Nature, and the nature of heaven. This is the clergyman's area of work and thinking.

The clergyman's ministry to the bereaved is limited by his parishioner's feelings toward him. If the pastor has failed in his ministry to the one who has died, particularly if that failure was due to his not calling during the illness, then his ministry to the family is apt to be ineffective. The minister who is disliked for any reason will not be helpful in this very intimate ministry regardless of his efforts. Thus, people often feel impelled to call another clergyman than their own minister in time of bereavement and they cannot understand a reluctance on the part of the one they call to respond to such a request. More people seem to be lost to the church because of the failure of the minister in bereavement than at any other time.

Another problem which crops up in bereavement, which many of our clergy overlook, is a feeling of guilt. This feeling may be justified through some failure on the part of the parishioner, or it may be imagined; in either case it is real to the sufferer and must be dealt with if relief is to be gained. For example, a woman whose husband had been a rural mail carrier came to her minister with the request that he drive with her over her deceased husband's mail route. She said he had always wanted her to ride with him on this trip but she had always put it off. Now that he was dead she realized she would never be able to fulfill his request; such a desire had laid hold upon her to make the trip that she could not sleep. When she had asked her children to take her for the drive they laughed at her and told her she was foolish.

The minister should have taken the trip with her; it would have been a half day well spent. But that should not have ended his work with her. After their trip she needed to be helped to understand why she had had such a desire; perhaps there were other feelings of guilt and failure in their married life which needed pastoral attention.

Whenever excessive mourning that holds over a long period of time is observed it is well to explore for guilt feelings. This may call for time and effort on the pastor's part. If the bereaved is a young widow there is some risk of a transfer of affection to the minister. The pastor who is young and inexperienced and who is not especially happy with his own wife will do well not to attempt a full ministry to a bereaved young widow. She has time and the healing forces of nature on her side so that she will be able to work out of her bereavement with the aid of mild encouragement on the part of the minister. The pastor's wife should not enter into this task of ministry to the bereaved any more than she should other pastoral tasks.

Immediately upon receiving word of the death of a parishioner the pastor should call at the home unless there is some request to the contrary. The family will usually arrange for him to see an immediate member of the family; circumstances will vary somewhat. During the early moments of such a call events will determine the minister's actions and remarks; it is a matter of following leads. The intimacy of the pastor's acquaintance with the family and the deceased and the nature of the death will determine the few questions the pastor asks. This will be followed by a discussion of arrangements for the funeral. If there is the desire on the part of the family to have another pastor take part in the service the minister may offer to call the other pastor and make arrangements. This offer is usually welcomed eagerly, thus embarrassment for all is avoided.

A prayer with the family should follow. There are few exceptions to this rule. The purpose of this prayer is to commend the spirit of the loved one to God's care and to remind the bereaved of God's care of them, which they are apt to forget at such a time. Following are several prayers for such an occasion, which may be adopted to the given situation.

Prayer Following the Death of a Child

Eternal God, Father of our Lord, Jesus Christ,
And Father of us all;
Our Lord has said, "Suffer the little children to come unto me,
And forbid them not, for of such is the kingdom of heaven";
He loved them as we have loved them,
We pray Thee, keep this one as we would keep him;
As our love has joined with Thy love in our care of him,
So we turn to Thee in this hour of need;
As Thou didst trust him in our care,
So we rest him in Thy care,
Knowing that Thou wilt keep this loved one
With a mother's love and a father's affection.
Strengthen these Thy children and comfort them,
May they find peace and courage in the days ahead,
And may they be reunited with this one
Through Jesus Christ, our Lord. AMEN

A Prayer Following the Death of a Mother

O Eternal God, in Whose Life we find our strength,
Through Whose Spirit we are renewed,
Grant us a sense of Thy nearness
That we may gain rest in Thee;

Thou knowest our needs at such a time as this,
Hear our prayers and make us strong again;
This one gone to Thee yet ever present in memory,
May we gain hope through her affection:
Devotion that counted not the cost, nor drew back at any sacrifice,
Keep her in Thy affection and may she not grow weary at the waiting,
Bless this child of her love; make it to grow strong in body and noble
    of spirit,
Bless this father and comfort him through the long hours,
Bless these loved ones and make them strong,
Through Jesus Christ, our Lord. AMEN

A Prayer Following the Death of an Aged Person

Almighty God, Source of life and Strength of faith,
Thou Who hast called us to our tasks and strengthened us,
Thou Who dost give us rest when the day's work is done;
We rejoice in a life well lived,
And in faith that is adequate to the day's task;
We give Thee thanks for the life of this one,
And for the lessons known from him;
Bless his loved ones and friends,
Reunite him with those gone before,
And may we look forward to the time
When we too will pass along this way,
Through Jesus Christ, our Lord. AMEN

In case the deceased is a non-parishioner and the pastor has a connection with him only through another member of the family, or where the community is small, the minister should call. He should follow the same general procedure as outlined above with the further specific statement to someone in the family, perhaps not the whole group, that he is willing to do anything possible to help but that no obligations should be felt on the part of the family to ask him to have a part in the service. Of all acts that are unbecoming a clergyman "corpse-chasing" is one of the greatest; at the same time this danger must not be permitted to block us out of performing our pastoral obligations to the bereaved.

The officiating clergyman may or may not go to the home immediately before the funeral. When he does he should have a prayer with the family before leaving for the church or funeral parlors. Following the formal funeral service the pastor should stay near the family until all have left the church or parlors, especially if the body is to be reviewed. The pastor, because he stands outside the family, can often help to quiet the already distraught feelings of the family by assisting those nearest the deceased. While in Texas I ministered to a thirty-five-year-old woman through her final illness. The family was large and closely knit. One sister was especially close to the deceased girl. As the family came to the casket at the end of the church service this sister broke down and refused to move on. I stepped up beside her, stood a moment, then placed my arm around her and walked with her out of the church to the waiting car. She went for me, she would not have gone as readily for anyone else.

There is a rapid trend away from the crude and non-Christian practice of viewing the body at the service, especially in the urban communities, just as there is a trend away from the practice of funeral sermons. The clergy can encourage this trend through conversation with the family. Some funeral directors recognize the desirability of keeping the casket closed during and after the service. Unfortunately many directors view their work as a business and not as an opportunity to be of service to suffering people; they believe their best advertisement is a well-displayed corpse which friends may admire, rather than a comforted family. We look toward the time when the non-Christian practice of worshipping dead bodies and cemeteries will have passed. The transition will be a slow one but there are some encouraging signs. More rapid progress could be made if clergy and funeral directors in given communities would sit down and discuss their mutual problems and practices in the light of the desire of both to be helpful to the bereaved. The clergyman can exert more influence upon funeral practices and consequently serve his people more effectively than he has bothered to do in most communities. Some pastoral associations have established committees to study this problem.

In planning a funeral service with a family Dr. Albert W. Palmer of Chicago Theological Seminary has pointed out, "Remember it is their funeral, not yours." A family should be permitted to have anything it wants in the way of music, hymns, scriptural reading, poetry, sermon or sermons. The purpose of the funeral service is to bring comfort to them; it is not an opportunity for a preacher to strike a blow at sinners he never sees except at such a time. There should be little basic difference in the service for a person who has committed suicide and the service for a faithful parishioner—for the most benevolent spirit or a poor beggar picked up beside the railroad track. The Christian message is a message of hope and it is our privilege to pronounce that hope at all times; it is best pronounced in the funeral service through selected scriptural passages and through prayer.

Important as the funeral service is the pastor's greatest opportunity to minister to the bereaved comes after the funeral in the immediate days that lie ahead when loneliness lays its heavy hand upon them. Some pastors follow the custom of calling once upon the bereaved and then going on about their work. This is a mistake. You cannot say that through one call you have completed your obligation or fulfilled your opportunity in ministering to the bereaved any more than one call upon a sick person is sufficient to meet the need there. Our pastoral work must be based upon the need of the parishioner, not on the whims or limited time of the pastor. The clergyman who does not have time to minister effectively to the bereaved does not have time to do anything else, and the words he utters in his next sermon will be nauseating to God and a blasphemy to Christ.

The underlying conditions of a ministry to the bereaved are the same as in all our ministry—the suffering of the parishioner, the emotional relationship or rapport between parishioner and pastor, the stability, faith, and quiet confidence of the pastor in the face of suffering. Over and above that his ministry to the bereaved will turn upon his skill; his skill in following leads, and his skill in asking questions; his wisdom in not asking certain questions, and his ability in interpretation, the delicacy of his reassurance, and the spiritual resources tapped through his prayer. All of which adds up to the fine art of pastoral work which is discussed later.

C. SPECIAL NEEDS

A special need that must be listed high in our scale of pastoral opportunities centers in the family where there is unemployment on the part of the breadwinner. This problem usually brings the parishioner to the pastor, but there are many times when the pastor must be the aggressor, due to embarrassment and hesitancy on the part of the family. Information concerning such a situation may reach the pastor through another parishioner or through a social worker. During the depression social workers often called the pastor of a family where there was a moral problem due to apprehension brought about by unemployment; more might have been called had those first clergymen succeeded in their task. We confidently believe that as the social worker and clergyman learn to work together in the future the pastor will be one of the first to be called by the social worker as problems arise concerning parishioners. See chapter XVI for further discussion of this problem.

Occasionally, even in the best of churches, parishioners go to jail. A young minister told me the story of one of his boys in the Young People's Department being put in jail because of a serious automobile accident for which he was responsible. The pastor sent the boy word that he was "behind him," but did not call at the jail lest his parishioners think he was taking the boy's part. We can imagine that the boy felt his pastor was so far "behind" him that it made no difference.

Most judges consider a pastor's interest a vital factor in determining the disposal of a problem which comes before them. The pastor needs to be intelligent in appealing to a judge and should remember that the judge has studied the problem and may know more than he does about the proper disposition of a charge. At the same time every judge knows that membership in a church where the minister is interested in his people is a stabilizing and constructive force in an individual's life.

D. The Aged and Shut-Ins

The aged and shut-ins are the most commonly neglected persons in our parishes; we take them for granted and day after day postpone our calls upon them. When we do call there seems to be little spiritual need present. Their conversation is repetitive as their lives are reasonably uneventful, and we are led to believe there are no spiritual needs present. We take their expressions of appreciation and their delight in our attention to them as flattering to ourselves instead of being an indication of their great loneliness. There is another reason, more definite, less flattering which constitutes the real reason why we postpone our calls upon these persons. Because of their condition they seem unlikely to make much contribution to the ongoing program of the church. I desire to be fair to the clergyman because I know just how many demands there are upon his time. Nevertheless, I know that the clergyman, like everyone else, does what he wants to do. We may conclude, therefore, that there is only one sound reason for the pastor's neglecting the aged and shut-ins—that is because he does not want to call upon them. All other reasons are just plain poppycock. In the making of these calls the true pastor's heart is tested, for the only reward from calling on this group is a spiritual reward. It is possible to test a clergyman's spiritual depth by inquiring if he calls upon his aged and shut-in persons.

The aged may be shut-in in that they cannot leave their homes, their rooms, their beds, or they may be able to go out for walks and do a few things about the home or farm. It calls for real imagination to keep an elderly person occupied and happy, and this task is not primarily the pastor's. At the same time, since his is the spiritual oversight of his people, he will be the one who will discover a miserable aged person whose family is concerned only with his physical well being and who have overlooked completely his loneliness. They often cannot understand why he is grouchy and unpleasant. The pastor may make suggestions as to how time and mind may be filled more interestingly so as to overcome that feeling of being unneeded and unwanted. He contributes to its relief insofar as he breaks the loneliness but he contributes more than the average person does in calling because he personalizes the faith that sustains an aged person in the evening hours of life. He represents in a unique way the life which is still ahead. Increasingly, as the aged person's friends cross over to the other life, as his body's strength drops away, as his thoughts turn to the life before him, he will want and need the encouragement of his pastor. Thus, while the minister in his calls will listen to the parishioner's recital of his day's events, small and of little consequence to the pastor but of great importance to the parishioner, he will also listen to the repeated recital of past experiences, and he must not fail to bring the comfort and reassurance of faith which is gained through prayer. It will be through the pastor's faith and through his Bible reading and prayer that this ministry of reconciliation will be carried on.

Many have noted the tendency of an aged person to live in the past and to speak of the past as the years move on. This is an easily understood tendency, for with the slowing up of the physical strength the mind reverts to the past and dwells upon the years of action. With the passing of time the stories often change also. Bishop Francis A. McConnell tells the story of an old uncle of his who was fond of reminiscing of his Civil War experiences. One particular story was told repeatedly and, as the years passed, it took on more and more glamour. In its original form the story was simply that Bishop McConnell's uncle had been sent out to search for food. He approached a smoke-house behind the Southern picket lines, but before the lock on the door could be forced a Southern patrol fired on him. However, he made his way back to his own lines and to safety. It was in this form that Bishop McConnell first remembered the story. But with the passing years first one man was killed and then another until the whole Southern patrol fell at the hand of the soldier. One day the Bishop said to the old man, "Uncle, I remember that story as you told it years ago. No one was killed in the story then. You were only fired on but escaped." The old man looked him over carefully then said with finality, "Frank, as I have grown older I find that my memory has grown better!"

These stories which the aged tell are not in themselves important. What is important is the emotional and spiritual satisfaction, the feeling of friendliness, which accompanies the telling. If loneliness is the major problem of the aged, and if loneliness is a sense of isolation, then the pastor has an important role to perform in preventing that sense of isolation from becoming too complete and absolute.

In Fort Smith, Arkansas, there is a club which is organized for the specific purpose of giving attention to the aged and shut-ins. Such a club has great possibilities.

Shut-ins may be elderly or they may be young or middle-aged persons who have had some physical handicap which limits their physical activity. This condition often does not limit their mental and spiritual activity but it frequently is permitted to. Occupational therapy works in this field and will become increasingly important in the future. Occupational therapy grew largely out of World War I; in World War II it is taking great strides forward in its work with veterans. A few communities, especially in New England, have employed therapists on a county and state basis who give attention to the rehabilitation of the physically handicapped. It is to be hoped that this practice will become general. The minister is in a position to aid in the establishing of this service in his community.

The clergyman should be informed as to what resources of this nature are available. Such information can be gained through the local family welfare society. When there is no trained personnel available, to carry on work both of diversion and rehabilitation with the shut-ins, especially with those less than sixty years of age, the clergyman may have to assume some responsibility in helping a parishioner make plans for the use of his time. A young man of thirty-three, who could not walk, needed encouragement to undertake a plan of selling stationery, Christmas cards and magazines. His improvement, mentally and spiritually, was marked from the day his plan got under way. Another man I knew had been handicapped seven years, being unable to leave his wheel chair, yet he was busy writing radio script. Another, a man who had lost both his legs, lived alone with his dog, doing all his own house work and cooking. He took great delight in training his dog to run errands and to do numerous tricks.

The problems of the handicapped are tremendous ones and the chief one is the isolation of loneliness. Newspapers, magazines, books, and the radio keep them in touch with the outside world and afford them entertainment. The radio especially makes a great contribution to the shut-in, but it is not enough. It is all in-going; for development spiritually and mentally there must be some out-going thought and activity. Some attention must be given to the fellowship which comes through belonging to the church visible. Visits by members of the church to the shut-ins can be planned and communion should be taken to them regularly.

E. New Members

Most persons will affiliate with the church only after contact with the pastor and many only after receiving instruction. We hope that the day is fast approaching when the practice of receiving uninstructed persons into full membership of the church will be a thing of the past. There are still many situations, however, when the invitation to membership is given to which persons who are unknown to the pastor will respond. This practice represents the weakness of the Protestant Church and should not be encouraged. Still it is done. In many situations it is possible to come into the church knowing little of its teaching, or history, and to understand little of its resources or practices.

When persons affiliate with the church who are unknown

to the pastor he should call upon them during the following week. While I was associate pastor at the Highland Park Methodist Church in Dallas it was my duty to make these calls. This church was growing so rapidly that keeping up with new member calls, along with the heavy pastoral load among the sick, bereaved, aged and shut-ins, was a difficult task. Dr. Marshall Steel, pastor of the church, followed the practice of holding new member receptions in his home, regularly and about fifty per cent of the new members responded to this invitation. While such a reception is not an adequate substitute for the pastoral call, still it is better than nothing. Actually it is a supplement to the pastoral call, for it brings new members into the pastor's home and affords them the opportunity of meeting other new members.

The pastoral call upon the new member is a get-acquainted call; it is parishioner-centered and should reveal the spiritual condition of the parishioner. This is an easy call to make and one which is emotionally satisfying to both persons. The call should be made in the home, preferably when both husband and wife are present if both have united with the church; otherwise calling upon more than one person is not as satisfactory and cannot be as effective as calling upon one person at a time. Many pastors follow the practice of taking their wives with them upon these calls. In general such a practice is at fault because the pastor-parishioner relationship is started on the wrong level: namely, that of a social visit. It has been my experience and that of pastors who have worked under my supervision, that at the first call the parishioner desires to talk about himself and his spiritual condition. This may be accomplished when more than two persons are present but every experienced pastor knows that it is difficult.

Some ministers are content to call upon husbands of families who have united with the church, saying that to become acquainted with and to hold the interest of the head of a family is the most important task we perform. Husbands and fathers are important and ministering to families is important but as pastors we are concerned with individuals and we must not be content until we have reached all the individuals who are under our spiritual guidance.

Further, there are more women who are emotionally unstable than there are men. That does not mean there are more psychotic women than men; the figure runs about equal. But outside the mental hospital women need more pastoral care than do men; because they seem to live more by their emotions. This is the result of several conditions, one being that emotionally the two sexes are just put together differently. The minister should not apologize because between sixty and eighty per cent of his pastoral work, both in his calling and in his office counseling, is done with women. If it is otherwise he should examine his work and his own anxieties.

The second purpose of this call is to help the member find his or her place in the ongoing program of the church. That does not mean he is to be drafted to teach a boys' Sunday School class immediately unless such is the request of a new parishioner who has had experience in such an activity. Neither should the call be for the purpose of finding out how large a contribution the parishioner plans to make to the church; wise is the pastor who leaves that to the members of the official board and who does not know the size of the contribution given members make.

I have found that until the pastor calls upon the new member the parishioner is not apt to feel he really belongs to the church. Not only should the pastor call upon the new members of a congregation but representatives of the official board, the women's society and church school should call as well. Perhaps not all should visit a given person or family, but whoever calls in addition to the pastor should be familiar with the work of the other organizations of the church.

A call by a lay member or members is no substitute for a call by the pastor. In fact, I do not think a call by the assistant or associate pastor is an adequate substitute for a call by the pastor, if the leading clergyman of a parish is really a pastor and not simply an administrator or preacher. Assistants can call upon prospective members, upon the sick, dying, aged and shut-ins, even upon the bereaved, but the wise pastor will call upon new members.

F. PROSPECTIVE MEMBERS

The church must constantly be alert to the ever-present task of enlisting new members. The evangelism of our fathers is passing. New methods must be substituted for the old.

Pastoral calling as a method of evangelism is not new. Our Lord spoke to certain ones saying, "Follow me." His followers have used that method through the generations by singling out certain individuals and saying, "I want you for Christ." Sometimes they have been successful and sometimes they have not, depending upon accompanying circumstances.

In their calling upon prospective members some pastors have thought that if they could out-talk the prospect he would be won. This out-talking often leads to arguing. The best way to convince a person he is right in an idea he holds is to argue with him that he is wrong. Any evangelistic effort which is based upon talking a person into the church is doomed to failure; you cannot argue people into the kingdom of heaven, any more than you can shout them in. That is why so much preaching is ineffective.

Our Lord used the method of love. The early church was founded upon fellowship; whenever it has forgotten that it has failed. We see organized religion popular wherever the church is founded upon fellowship, regardless of the theology it teaches. Perhaps love is what religious people have in common, after all.

Pastoral work, as I am describing it, is founded upon love. (See chapter IX.) The pastor's method in calling upon prospective members is the same as it is upon his parishioners. He does not need to tell people why he calls unless it is to reassure them concerning his interest in them; they know that he is a clergyman and as such is interested in their spiritual welfare. To bring the subject of church membership to their attention and to bring them hurriedly to a decision concerning their spiritual condition is like proposing to a young lady upon first acquaintance.

There are many people who have been reared in families where there is little or no love between mother and father, consequently there is little sound affection for the youngster. These youngsters as they become adults will be suspicious of affection and will have little comprehension of the fellowship of the church in Christ; the grace of God will be beyond their understanding. They often succeed in marrying fine young men and women only to lead their husbands and wives a miserable life because, basically, they are miserable themselves. They lack security at the point where they should feel most secure; they do not know how to love or be loved. The pastor, calling upon such persons, faces the difficult task of demonstrating God's interest in them which can best be done through his own affection for them.

The main purpose of the call upon the prospective member is to express an interest in the person and to overcome any hesitancy which may be felt on the prospect's part toward the church. Such a call should offer the opportunity to ask any questions concerning the beliefs and practices of the church which may be in the prospect's mind. If there are children in the home who are in the church school they will be a subject of conversation. Many parents will come to church with their children when an interest is taken in them by the pastor.

I understand that of the converts made by the Roman Catholic Church, thirty per cent first became interested through care received in some hospital run by the Roman Catholics. This proves that when a person is in difficulty and receives help he is impressed by those who help him. Love begets love; interest begets interest. Illness and suffering should not be taken advantage of for purposes of evangelism; at the same time we know that suffering, as described above, opens doors for pastoral care, and out of pastoral care arises the desire for continued fellowship in the church. A man who had been sick for some time and upon whom we had called regularly for ten months sent for me one day. He said, "You fellows have been so decent to me. I'd like to get on your books. I'd like to join your church. How do I go about it?" He did not need to be told why we had called upon him. He knew that as individuals we would not have even known of his illness had we not been ministers.

Calling upon prospective members is a matter of establishing a rapport, a matter of listening, of taking time. There will be a response when there is a need on the part of the prospect; when there is no need present any amount of persistence and argument will be to no avail.

Transferring a personal loyalty to the larger loyalty of Christ and God and the church is one of the most delicate tasks we face as pastors, and one in which we commonly fail. This fact is more generally true among the free church denominations than among the liturgical denominations. One Sunday morning I was told by a member of the official board of a large church in a Southern city that people had come as far as "twenty miles" that morning just to hear Dr. Blank preach because of their affection for him; there was no mention of their love for the church into which he had brought them. Such a statement indicates the limitations of that pastor's ministry, yet his board and his brethren would think of him as one of the most effective ministers in the whole state of Alabama.

Two or three things can be said conclusively upon this problem. First, in those churches where preaching is emphasized this problem is more acute than in traditions where preaching is not prominent, such as the Roman Catholic and the Episcopal churches, especially the Anglo-Catholic wing. I have often heard members of one of these churches express criticism of their clergy, yet their loyalty to the church never wavered. In some of our Protestant churches if the members do not like the clergyman they absent themselves from the church and may never return. As Protestants we have claimed "the message" characterizes our tradition, therefore the pulpit has been placed in the center of the church. The trend now is to place the cross and the altar in the center of the church and the pulpit at the side. Symbolically this is a great step forward.

Secondly, more careful instruction of our people before they are received into the church should help to overcome this problem of transferring the personal loyalty into the larger loyalty. This involves instruction in the history of the church, its sacraments, symbols and practices, and an actual follow-up to be certain that those who need it are oriented in the fellowship of the church.

In light of my contention that loneliness is the great emotional problem of our time, the strengthening of the spirit of fellowship is one of the greatest evangelistic attractions the church has; at the same time this fellowship must be God centered or it deteriorates into a club or an association of persons of goodwill.

G. The Routine Call

I can think of no adequate term to describe the average, every-day call which is made upon parishioners regardless of their spiritual needs and without specific purpose in the way of church organizational promotion. For want of a better term I shall call them *routine* calls. This call is made for no other reason and with no other excuse than that a given person is a member of a given church. In some respects this is the most effective and most appreciated call the pastor makes because he calls of his own volition; not because someone is sick or bereaved, and not to promote some program or make some request. This is the kind of calling upon which the church of another generation was founded. When older parishioners bemoan the passing of "the good old days" in the church or when they speak of "the grand old pastors," it is this type of call that they are talking about. Just how much of it was done in "the good old days" I have been unable to ascertain because reminiscences of the past have a tendency to take on an exaggerated glamour. Whether our fathers in the faith actually succeeded in carrying on such work extensively or not is unimportant; that they did more than we are doing we may be sure. Such calls are the heart of pastoral work, the foundation stones, the mother and father, the essence, the alpha and omega all wrapped into one.

The routine call serves two purposes: it builds up rapport between pastor, people and God, and it puts the pastor in position to discover spiritual and emotional needs in an incipient stage before they have become serious problems.

As we shall see presently in chapter IX, the emotional rapport between pastor, parishioner and God is one of the underlying conditions that makes for effective pastoral work. Without this satisfying feeling of friendliness the pastor does harm when the parishioner is suffering. To establish this feeling is difficult or impossible unless the parishioner believes you are interested in him, and unless he believes the pastor is interested he is not apt to think that God is. The most common rebuke faced by the officers of the church when collecting money is that "the church is not interested in me." By the church is usually meant "the minister," although when laymen call upon other members in the name of the church the failure of the pastor is overlooked. In one respect no other caller can take the place of the pastor, for he represents the church and God in a unique sense. We are often impatient with parishioners who assume the attitude, "The church is not interested in me"; we think and sometimes say, "Are you interested in the church?" This is an unfair attitude. The church is a fellowship. The Christian movement grew out of a little group of people collected around Jesus who had sought them out saying, "Follow me." He was the aggressor. It was much later, after months and years of teaching, working and living together that "the message" or "gospel" of Jesus came to mean much to them. In fact it seems to have been only after Jesus had died and risen from the dead that they became an ongoing fellowship who were interested in proclaiming his "gospel" and even then they were such a loosely knit, quarreling, strong-headed lot that Jesus had to give them leadership of a strong and personal nature for a long time. Then only a few seemed to grasp the meaning of his message; most of them were concerned with his life and personality. Perhaps we should remember the slowness of those early Christians to grasp his message when we become impatient with the church. It was not his message but his personality that caught their loyalty and held it. It was his pastoral touch, his personal interest in them that attracted and held them. That is the basis upon which rapport is founded. It is also the essence of pastoral work.

The second significant reason for the routine call is that the pastor is able to discover incipient needs before they become serious beyond the point of remedy. The physician is always bemoaning the fact that patients delay seeing a doctor when a suspicious lump, pain or lesion does not heal. When months later a physician's help is sought he discovers that a cancer which could have been taken care of easily when it was first noticed by the patient is now past surgical treatment. The same thing is true in the spiritual field. With so many of our people unhappily married, some of whose problems could be overcome through counseling, we need to be constantly alert for difficulties. Most of our counseling in the marital field, especially at the outset of our work with a given family, will start with the wife. Therefore calling in the home, if the pastor is alert and skillful, will uncover some of these difficulties before the marriage is seriously threatened. In its various phases the pressures of human suffering, especially apprehension, will come easily to the pastor's attention when he is available and has the spiritual welfare of his people at heart, as contrasted with the all too common clergyman who is concerned with the church program but forgets the people.

I am conscious of the fact that the pastor is not an expert in all the problems he comes across, neither is the general physician in his field, neither is the public health nurse, neither is the teacher. But the pastor, like the doctor, knows that eighty per cent of the problems he faces will straighten out with a little help and encouragement. We recognize that without that help and encouragement, small as it may seem, many of those eighty per cent will develop into serious, perhaps irreparable trouble. There are probably ten per cent who cannot be helped at all, regardless of who tries. There are the ten per cent, as a rough guess, who need help, expert help, and it becomes the pastor's responsibility to get them to someone who can supply that help. In many instances he will be able to cooperate in the treatment. This would be true in the case where the pastor discovers a mother worrying about a behavior problem in a child. She should be directed to a good child psychologist if one is available, but the pastor should follow up the referral to see if there is some marital difficulty present which he could help in resolving. This follow-up should be with the psychologist or social worker to whom the mother has gone, then with the mother herself.

The couple who desires to adopt a baby will often speak of it to the pastor. The finding and selection of a baby for a given couple is a highly skilled practice which social work has explored. The pastor's task is one of referring the couple to the proper agency and of supplying character references to the agency. Some pastors believe that adopting a baby will straighten out a marital situation. That is a terrific burden to place upon the shoulders of a baby who needs all the security two persons who love each other can give him. A good child-placing agency will not permit a baby to be adopted by a couple who are trying to save their marriage through such a procedure. The pastor should not recommend adopting a baby upon that basis.

Another situation which the pastor will meet in his routine calling occurs in the family where there is a handicapped child who needs to be placed in a special school for his own sake, for the sake of other children in the family, and for the sake of the parents. This is a delicate situation and calls for the greatest of tact and skill on the part of the pastor. A handicapped child, in his dependence and need for greater care, almost always claims an undue amount of affection from the mother so that he fails to develop emotionally. This seriously affects the mother's relationship with other children in the family and affects the mother's and father's relationship with each other. The family where there is a handicapped child deserves a special place on the clergyman's list of those needing extra pastoral care. A pastor can always secure information concerning a school for handicapped children from social workers.

A woman came to our hospital as a patient herself because she was worried about her child who had recently been placed in such a school. I obtained all the information I could from a social worker concerning the school in order to establish my authority with the mother so that I could reassure her. Then I began to search for a guilt feeling concerning her child. The guilt feeling was finally revealed and the mother seemed to improve.

Since all of us have experiences buried away that we are trying to forget there are hidden guilt feelings in most of us. A peculiar experience, such as having a handicapped child, crystallizes into personal blame, regardless of the fact that our feelings had nothing to do directly with the child. The child's suffering is thought of as a "visitation from God" for the mother's sins, therefore she thinks of it as her "cross." Strange thinking, indeed, and a commentary upon how little of the New Testament and of Jesus' understanding of God as the Loving Father is really accepted by our people. Because of this peculiar tie-up between the family problem and the mother's attitude toward God, the pastor may be especially helpful in this situation. He will fail if he rushes in and gives a superficial opinion, but if he is genuinely interested in such a family he may, after much patient waiting and watching, be of help.

Another problem the pastor will strike in his routine calling is the one encountered where a young couple is living with the parents of one or the other. This is an abnormal situation and one which is to be discouraged. The time to hit this problem hardest is in pre-marital counseling. When I am asked to marry a couple and after I have gone over the marriage service I inquire, "What are your plans, where will you live?" If the young couple plan to live with parents I ask, "Why?" They are open to counsel at that time and they will appreciate your interest so long as they recognize that it is in their behalf. It is easier to save a situation then than later. Wherever I find a couple already living with parents I am especially alert. I can tell in an instant how things are when I see how the mother-in-law treats the son-in-law or the mother treats the daughter. Sometimes, not often, we are surprised to find that it actually works. I met a fine young couple in an Alabama town who lived with the wife's family, having no children of their own. When I was introduced to the father-in-law he said, "Paul is the favored member of this family so far as my wife is concerned." Paul explained, "I said to my wife, if she ever divorces me she'll have to move because I won't leave this family." His wife said, "I often accuse Paul of marrying me so that he might live with my family. He just asked my mother what daughter she had, and since my sister was married he said I'd do. It didn't matter much anyway as long as he got to live with my mother." The average instance of living with parents, regardless of the cause, is not that happy.

The more frequent situation is the parent or parents living with the son's or daughter's family. This may work out better than the young couple living with the parents, but there is considerable strain involved. The strain is greatest upon the children growing up in the family on the one side and upon the grandparents on the other. There is always the struggle between the generations. It is bad enough between those immediately adjacent, such as parents and children; the conflict between grandparents and grandchildren is even greater because the gap is wider in point of years, energy, customs and interests. That is why grandparents spoil grandchildren so frequently. They either refuse to undergo the strains of disciplining the youngsters or they over discipline them.

The pastor, calling in a home where the mother has come to live with the daughter's family, should be especially alert. Under proper conditions of privacy a simple question such as, "How does your mother get along with your children? Do they bother her?" may bring a story of apprehension from your parishioner. Maybe she has not felt she could talk with her husband; maybe he has been arguing with her upon the subject; maybe he has leaned over backward to avoid being critical, as some husbands will—believe it or not—and the wife has not gained help from him. She needs to talk to someone who will be objective and strengthen her in her decision that for the benefit of all concerned, especially for her own children, her mother should be encouraged to live somewhere else. Many a sensitive daughter permits her mother to live in her home, disrupting the lives of her children and herself because another less sensitive brother, sister or relative has told her she should look after her mother. A little quiet encouragement on the part of the pastor may be the determining factor in working out a better plan. Again, I suggest that you use all the tact and patience you have, in working in this situation.

As a result of traveling about the country, consulting with chaplains, civilian clergy, and social workers, I am convinced that the mother-son attachment is not only one of the most serious psychological problems we have but one of the most common. Every clergyman ought to preach, at least once a year, on the general subject, "The Art of Being a Mother-in-law." Since he himself will never be one he ought to be sufficiently objective to do a "rugged" job on the subject. The ability to permit our youngsters to grow up is a most difficult one, because we cling to the past; we know the road over which we have come and the uncertain future which lies ahead.

A mother wrote an Army chaplain saying, "My son does not answer my letters. Recently I sent him a camera and he did not even thank me." The chaplain found the man was making a good record as a soldier. When he talked with him about his failure to write home the soldier said, "I am determined to pay her back for all the selfish cruelty she has dumped on me all my life. She's always treated me like a baby." Another man refused to see his mother, although she had traveled a thousand miles to visit him at his camp. He also was making a good record in the service. Both of these men had belatedly recognized their poor emotional equipment for the hard, man's job before them and both of them correctly blamed their mothers for failing to help them to become men. What they further failed to do was to recognize why their mothers had tried to tie the boys closely to them emotionally. These women were both emotionally starved, frustrated persons themselves.

Unfortunately not all sons are as well off emotionally as these two men. They knew they must break away and were doing it; both were making good records in the service and with some encouragement would be all right. Probably thousands of the problems of the psychoneurotics discharged from the service have turned upon this problem of having failed to grow up emotionally due to the mother's emotional immaturity. We place the blame upon the mother because the child comes most under her influence during the formative years of its early life as Dr. Karl Menninger points out in his book, *Love against Hate*. Many mothers would say readily, "Well, I saved my son from the Army anyway." Yes, saved him; and for what? Years of agony—years of knowing he could not play a man's part in a time of national crisis. He is saved for the mental hospital.

This problem crops up in the mother-in-law influence in broken marriages. Recently I was consulted by the pastor of a girl whose husband is serving with the armed forces abroad. The boy and girl had met and carried on their courtship during the quiet months of the first year of the emergency before the United States got into the war. They planned their marriage and the boy's mother arrived from a distant city two days before the wedding. She tried desperately to get the young couple to postpone the wedding for no good reason; in this she failed. She attended the wedding but did not attend the reception. A few weeks after the wedding the husband was ordered abroad. For a while letters to the wife arrived regularly, then they became less frequent and their tone became more formal and less affectionate. At the time the wife consulted her minister the husband had changed his allotment from his wife to his mother, and the wife had not heard from him for two months. "How would you have dealt with that wife?" the pastor asked. First I would have let her talk, as my friend did. Then I would ask her how she felt about it all, giving her a chance to pour out her bitterness, her disappointment, her hope. Then I would ask what chance she thought she had in winning her husband's love back and if she cared to try in the face of odds against her. If she did want to try I would suggest that she come to see me again soon to talk further. I would urge her to keep in touch with me as future developments unfolded. Certainly I would keep in touch with her. If, however, she had said she did not think she had much chance of resurrecting her marriage I would agree. She does not have. In fact, her mother-in-law has won her *dear* son back and I would let her have him if I were the girl, but perhaps she does not feel that way. After all, she is the one who is married to him. Therefore I would be careful to avoid telling her the show is over, even though I believed it was.

Sex plays an important role in building the emotional foundations of a marriage and in prying son away from mother during the early months of marriage until new emotional habits can be formed and a husband can get used to his wife, who is different from mother. This is the advantage a wife has in the struggle against her husband's mother. In the above instance the wife lost the struggle because her husband was ordered overseas so soon after the wedding, thus causing a separation which gave the mother odds in the struggle.

A minister in counseling with a wife concerning her marital situation which was going badly suggested that she go to the beauty parlor and "get the works," then go to a store and buy the most attractive nightgown she could find. What other suggestions he made as to campaign strategy I do not know. The result was that the husband secured a vacation due him and took his wife on a second honeymoon. It is amazing that as smart as women are they still can overlook the obvious. I suppose it is because some of them still believe they are sought out for their virtues.

A similar story that came to my attention concerned a school teacher of thirty-five who sought her minister's counsel. Since she was unmarried her older brother had suggested that their mother and father live with her which worked well for some time, until the girl awakened to the fact that life was slipping away from her and that she wanted a home and family of her own. The girl was dressed in the drab conservative outfit that school teachers usually wear; her hair was a bit frowzy; her face, hands and nails had that look that having to take care of other people's children give them. The minister inquired if other plans could be made for her parents so that she could be independent; yes, they could. He inquired if she had saved any money; yes, she had. He suggested that she go to the beauty parlor and get everything in the book, facial, hair-do, manicure; then she was to go to the best women's store in the city and buy the finest outfit she could buy. After that they would talk again. A few Sundays later the minister looked up at the beginning of his service to see a strikingly beautiful woman walk proudly down the aisle and take a seat well to the front of the church. Not until she looked up at him and smiled sweetly did he recognize the formerly drab girl who had consulted him a few weeks before. Needless to say he worked at a disadvantage that morning as he watched the members of the congregation when they began to recognize the girl. Little did they know their pastor's part in that personality transformation. The next time he was called upon to consult with that girl was in regard to plans for her wedding! If only all our pastoral work could have such a happy ending.

Another problem we encounter in our routine calling which might not otherwise come to our attention is the marital difficulty. This is perhaps the most common problem among our people and yet it is one which the average clergyman is missing. We are missing it because of the guilt feelings that are involved in marital trouble, and since the clergyman, in a subtle sense, is the chief spark plug of guilt feelings, his help is sought only when a person feels she has a clear-cut case of marital failure on the husband's part. An experienced and wise minister estimated that twenty-five per cent of his parishioners were happily married and he thought that was a generous estimate. I agree, it *is* generous. Another minister I know feels strongly that unless the church becomes realistic and effective in the field of better preparing its people for marriage and in marriage counseling we will fail utterly in the years ahead. A leading physician of Boston believes that the church must assume the burden of such work because the medical profession will not, due to its conservatism. I will speak more of marital counseling later in chapter VI but just let me say here that the opportunity to be of help in marital counseling will come to us when we have demonstrated we can be helpful. Even then most of our opportunity will come as we make ourselves available in routine calling, and as we discover these problems early through such calling. It is for this reason above all else that I believe in calling in the home and calling alone. Ninety per cent of our marital counseling originates with the wife.

A few simple questions are sufficient. "How are things going?" "How is Joe?" "How are the children?" Time must be given to allow an answer to these questions. Watch for what is not said. Watch for apologies. Watch for failure to quote husband, watch for apologies for not having been to church. Joe works so hard! So do other people! People come to church when they want to, just as they do other things that they want to do. Watch for the vague statement, "We've been having a hard time," and the curious avoiding of your eyes, the restless hands—then wait! The story will come in good time.

Closely following the marital difficulty which the pastor discovers in routine calling is the situation where the husband is drinking heavily but the wife is doing nothing about it but worry and nag. She has spoken to no one but she desperately needs to talk about it. The husband's problem is not limited to himself any more than a youngster's problem can be understood apart from his home and what goes on there. The fact that many wives realize this prevents them from seeking help —that plus a false sense of loyalty to the husband. The pastor can do little to help such a family until there has been suffering enough to cause the wife really to want help; often this does not happen until the situation is quite out of hand. The wife may have lapsed into the habit of using sickness to manipulate her husband and while he may acquiesce for a while, finally he rather blindly and desperately turns to drink and then to the "understanding" secretary. The pastor stumbles into such a situation; the wife pours out her feelings to him and he goes home to brood and ponder over the story.

I would suggest a consultation with the wife's physician as a first step, also that you keep the story to yourself. If you must talk to someone about it, talk to God. Do not burden your wife with these stories—she has enough to do looking after you without having to serve as a relief valve. The doctor will not tell you much until you reveal something of your insight into the situation, then he will either discourage you by assuring you that he knows the whole story and that nothing can be done or he will dump the whole problem in your lap by saying that only you and God can do anything constructive. Occasionally you will meet a really intelligent physician who is not too tired, who will discuss the situation reasonably and will welcome you as an ally. If so, you have cause to rejoice.

Secondly, I would call upon the husband casually and seek to gain his goodwill. In the light of your reception by him you can judge how far you should go in revealing your understanding of the situation. If a woman has retreated into illness years before because she is afraid of sex or because she seeks attention and sympathy, it is doubtful that you will be able to do much, especially unless you do it in cooperation with the physician, and usually he will have to bear the brunt of the treatment. Your task will be that of support. Do not expect to be effective often with such a problem.

There are a half dozen causes for a husband's drinking. I am not thinking of heavy drinking now. Heavy drinking, alcoholism, is a disease that needs medical treatment just as much as heart disease does. Even then there is little chance of the patient receiving much help; perhaps one in fifty can be reclaimed. But the average husband who drinks not as a social experience with the boys but as an escape, who is endangering his home, his job, his position in the community, does so for one of several reasons: "relative trouble," lack of sexual compatibility with his wife, guilt feelings in his attitude toward his wife, difficulty in his job which he cannot absorb because of lack of support from his wife, criticism and nagging from an overly ambitious and jealous wife. All of these reasons tie up with the wife herself, and seem unfair to womanhood. They are unfair if judged in an absolute sense, but women are shrewder than men; therefore the secret to solving man's problems is through women. What you, as a clergyman, can do with this problem will depend upon the desire for help on the wife's part and upon how astute you are.

Another difficulty you will come across in routine calling is sickness where a physician has not been called for various reasons: fear of what will be found, the belief that health will soon return without a doctor's help, lack of knowledge in knowing whom to call, dislike of a former physician, inability to pay a doctor's bill. If it is a problem of attitude toward a doctor you may have a difficult time. If it is lack of finances there will be persons to whom you can turn for help. You will also know what hospitals nearby do free work. Often it will be a matter of contacting a specialist through another clergy friend in a larger city so that a crippled child, or a person who needs special attention, may receive it.

It is a delicate task suggesting that a person should change physicians but the clergyman should know that a family has the right to ask for a consultation (the opinion of another physician), and the attending physician is ethically obligated to agree to such a request. Any doctor who objects to having a consultation is one to be suspicious of and dismissed as soon as possible. Also the clergyman should be aware of the fact that the family can discharge a physician whenever they do not like the way a case is being handled. Sometimes a family will not know that. Ordinarily it is the clergyman's task to support the physician and usually this can be done honestly, but doctors are human beings and are subject to the same human frailties as other people. Not all doctors are good doctors, and the clergyman will often have to carry some responsibility in counseling with a family about the medical attention a patient is receiving.

Closely associated with the need for a physician which the pastor may discover is the need for a registered or practical nurse. Sometimes it is simply a matter of calling the public health nurse and asking her to call for a few minutes a day. Again, it may be that a registered nurse may be needed to briefly supplement a practical nurse's work. My wife, a graduate nurse, gave a very sick girl a shampoo, which was what she wanted and needed more than she needed prayer. After the shampoo the prayer was much more helpful. The pastor, calling regularly, will discover these things; he must and will know many people who have many skills but do not know of specific needs as he does. Much of a social worker's task is in knowing a community's resources and in getting these to people who need them. In this respect the clergyman does the same thing as he goes about among his people.

A common problem the pastor encounters in his routine calling is the need of the handicapped for rehabilitation counsel and training. A similar problem is the loneliness of the shut-in and aged. A young pastor told me of a parishioner who said, "I have been shut in for six weeks and not a person from the church has been to see me besides yourself." The pastor knew that she was not a friendly person herself, but he spoke to two or three members without revealing the above statement, and suggested that they call upon her. Both patient and visitors derived deep satisfaction from the visit.

The pastor will also discover unemployment in his routine calling. Sometimes he can do something about this and sometimes he can't. Each pastor ought to have a business friend or an acquaintance in an employment agency to whom he can turn. In Dallas we sent our people who were seeking employment to the director of the Community Chest who had his hand on the pulse of the community needs for employment. A young man who had been discharged from the Army was discouraged because he could not get a job. I was able to interpret his discharge in such a way that he had a job within two days.

The talented youngster who needs to go to college and receive special training but cannot afford it will come to the attention of the pastor. The girl who wants to become a nurse but knows little about training schools, the boy who wants to be a mechanic but whose parents want him to be an attorney, the girl who is interested in people, but does not want to be a doctor or nurse and who cannot become a minister, may never have heard of social work and know nothing of social work schools—all these and many others come to the attention of the pastor as he goes about the parish making routine calls.

If the pastor waits for these needs to come to him few of them will ever come. He finds them; his help is accepted because he has demonstrated his interest in his people by actually going to them. It is more than talk, it is a demonstration. I know many consecrated clergymen who have excellent ideas about church promotion who are literally working themselves to death with promotion work; their sermons are well thought out and effectively delivered; yet their ministries are failing. Their people have gotten the idea the pastor is not interested in them and they are right. He is interested in Christ, he is interested in bringing people to God, he is interested in welfare work for the poor. He is *not* interested in his own parishioners. If someone comes to him for help he will work his heart out; his parishioners know that but still they feel cool toward him. One thing he fails to do: *he does not ring door bells;* he does not go to the people!

I have spent a good deal of time trying to develop a plan which the pastor may follow in his routine calling that will carry him to all his parishioners. Most pastors who do this kind of calling simply go from house to house contacting those parishioners who live on a given street. Others follow the alphabetical listing of their parishioners. The limitation of the house-to-house calling is that certain members of the family are seen but others are not.

There is a plan followed by the Reverend John A. Davidson of Selma, Alabama, which seems to be the most far-reaching of all. It is so simple it is no wonder we have overlooked it, that is, the *birthday plan*. It is his practice to list the birthdays of every member of the congregation as they come into the church. Dr. Davidson then writes a letter upon the day of the birthday and follows it with a call within a week. The letters are not form letters and he varies each as he can and as he has some special comment or word of appreciation he wishes to express to a given parishioner. This plan includes the youngsters as well as the adults. Naturally, many a pre-school age child would not especially understand the purpose of such a call but none would be more appreciative. It was said of the great physician, Dr. Wm. Osler of Johns Hopkins, that he had the ability to gain the confidence of a child. He often got down on the floor and played with his small friends.

The birthday plan has the advantage of carrying the pastor

to the husband as well as the wife. I do not emphasize the importance of calling in the home just because so much of our work is with women; it should not be disproportionate with either women or men. But there is something sacred about one's home and the pastor's call there will have more significance than it ever could in an office, a store, or a factory.

The pastor goes to his people

CHAPTER VI

THE PEOPLE COME TO THE PASTOR

A. Pre-Marital Counseling

FOREMOST among counseling problems which come to the pastor are those couples who are to be married. To be sure, they seek the pastor's help for the ceremony of marriage, with little thought of more than a conference about the ritual itself. To go further into a discussion of some of the factors that make for a successful marriage calls for tact and judgement. But our people are so poorly prepared for marriage that some pastors feel the clergy must assume major responsibility in the field if the church is not to fail its people in the area of the home.

Marriage may be considered successful when the affiliation contributes positively to the personalities of the two parties, thus enabling them to make their own contribution in the wise and affectionate rearing of their children. As a conservative estimate it is safe to say that only about ten per cent of our people are happily married; that does not mean that all the others are complete failures. This high degree of failure in marriage reveals that something is seriously wrong so far as our marriage practices are concerned. A regime of suppression, moralism and preachments will make no contribution to this problem. We have had that. The alternative of education, enlightenment and understanding holds some hope. At least it has not been tried.

The clergyman is in a strategic position in relation to the marriage problem and many are carrying on counseling in the field. Ideally the pastor should discuss the emotional and spiritual forces which go to make up a successful marriage and refer the couple to a physician for information upon family planning and the art of sexual happiness. Many pastors, particularly the younger clergy, serving in small communities, will not have a physician in the community who is well enough informed to carry his part of this counseling problem. Rather than trying to carry the whole load himself the pastor should contact a physician in a larger town who is capable of doing this work. Such a contact can be made through a pastor friend who will know the physicians in his community. In normal times a drive of a hundred miles or farther is not unreasonable for such counsel.

Secondly, where there is no doctor who is equipped to work in the field of birth control and sex education, the pastor may cultivate such an interest in his doctors and urge them to assist in this type of counseling. Some physicians will be reluctant, especially where there is considerable public opinion against the spreading of family planning information but when the pastor refers couples to the physician for examination and counsel most doctors will cooperate. No girl should be married without an examination, for many a distressing experience and ultimate shipwreck of a home may be avoided by a few simple suggestions. The pastor cannot urge such an examination too strongly.

Further, the pastor may put certain literature into the couple's hands when they come seeking his services for marriage. There are many books available. Some may be loaned, others given outright. Some ministers give Foster Wood's little book, "Harmony in Marriage," to every couple they marry.[1]

[1] Federal Council of Churches, New York. 50 cents.
  Ideal Marriage, Van DeVelde. $7.50. Random House, New York. Is the great classic in this field.

Pre-marital counseling should include a consideration of th
couple's plans for their own home. If they plan to live wit
parents the pastor may question this decision. While such
question may be considered none of his business, still his inter
est will be appreciated. No healthy, normal couple will wan
to live with their in-laws, but for some reason such may b
the plan. The pastor's suggestions to the contrary may b
sufficient to influence them to make another decision. I woul
not be insistent upon this point unless there was some re
question already in the minds of the couple.

The pastor is called upon to marry many persons who ar
not members of his church and here the question should b
raised about what plans they are making for a church hom
The couple may not do anything about it at the time but th
thought will have been planted in their minds. Five or si
years later concern for their own youngster may bring ther
to church.

A young physician and his prospective bride were makin
arrangements for their wedding. The bride was a Roma
Catholic, the bridegroom a Methodist. The doctor was still i
training and they had not decided where they would live. I sai
"What about your church home? With your background i
will be easy to let it slip. While the two of you may be conten
as you are now, you will have to decide about your children.
They said they would like to be together in whatever churc
they selected. The girl said, "I will be anything but a Meth
odist." This remark was made because her prospective mother
in-law, a Methodist, was very intolerant toward the Roma
Catholic Church. I suggested they consider the Episcopa
Church. This was a happy compromise since it meant bot
would make some move from the religion of their childhoo
which would avoid one or the other making all the conces
sions, as usually happens.

As clergymen we should make an effort to follow up the couples we have married. This may be done through a personal call periodically and especially upon or near the date of their anniversary, or through a letter. Too often we have married our young people, pocketed our fee and gone merrily on our way, accepting no further responsibility and failing to see a further opportunity to be of service to those who honor us by seeking our blessing upon one of the few really great experiences of their lives.

B. MARITAL COUNSELING

As I have indicated elsewhere more of our people suffer from marital difficulties than from any other single problem. The limitation of this observation is that marital difficulties are never isolated but are an infinite number of interrelated problems; yet for purposes of analysis we may be permitted to over-simplify the actual condition. A large number of wives will say to you simply, "My husband and I are having trouble." This is the presenting symptom. It is up to the pastor to dig out the underlying causes in order to help the parishioner understand the difficulty.

There are several ways in which the pastor may work into the area of marital counseling. The first is to prepare himself for it and to be sure his attitude is one that will be helpful. If he is prejudiced toward the institution of marriage because of his own failure in marriage, or if he is concerned at the high divorce rate, then he will fail in his counseling in this field. The divorce rate is too low in light of the number of unhappily married people there are. There have been many studies made of the problem of marriage, but even so most of the work remains to be done upon this subject, for we know so little about what makes a good marriage. What marital counseling is done

is largely hit or miss but even that is better than running away
from the task as some of our clergy do.

Due to the intimate and often unflattering personal nature
of marital counseling many of our people prefer to seek help
from strangers. It is a matter of saving face. What man wants
to admit he is ignorant of the emotional make-up of woman?
Yet, woman herself is ignorant of her own make-up. Many a
girl has fought shy of sex and of petting until she was married
only to find that the reading of a wedding ceremony did not
change her basic attitude toward sex and men; in marriage she
was still afraid of them. The result is that sex to her is abhor-
rent. After a week or a month or a year, depending upon how
smart she is, she recognizes that her husband's attitude toward
her is changing but she does not know, or will not admit, why.

What woman likes to admit she has married a little boy who
is still tied closely to his mother's apron strings? She does her
best to break the tie but fails. Even in seeking counsel she
often refuses to admit that she has failed; she tries to cover
up her husband's infantilism out of loyalty to him and out of
her own pride in herself.

These conditions all combine to prevent wives from seeking
pastoral help as well as sending them off to someone else for
counsel. The pastor who reveals some understanding of the
underlying problems that make for marital discord either in
his preaching or in his talks to groups will have marital counseling to do.

The pastor who is not happily married himself will not work
effectively in this field. Since the number of our pastors who
are happily married would seem to vary little from the average,
we may expect comparatively few ministers to be effective
marital counselors. The same thing is more true of social workers for most of them have never even been married.

Every pastor will, however, have some people who come to

im for help because of marital unhappiness. He can carry
hrough on the first phase of such counseling; he can listen
passively. If the pastor feels uncomfortable while doing this
work he should have enough interest in his parishioners to refer
hem to someone who can be of help.

In marital counseling the first task is to get the story of
immediate unhappiness. This may be done with a few simple
questions and some reassurance such as, "Feel free to talk
frankly. You may be sure I will keep your confidence." When
here are tears, as tears there usually are, a statement of reassurance such as, "Do not feel hurried, we have plenty of
time," will help. Further questions as, "How long has this been
going on?" "Have you ever been happy with your husband?"
"How long did you know each other before you were married?"
"How did you come to fall in love with each other?" "What
was the attitude of your family, of your husband's family,
toward the match?" "What kind of home did you have? Were
your mother and father happily married?" "Were your husband's mother and father happily married?" "How do you
know?" "Did you have other boy friends before your husband?" "Did he have other girl friends?" "How did you think
about marriage as you were growing up?" "What did you
expect from marriage?" "Are your marital relations satisfying?" "What did you know about sex when you were married?" "If your marital relations are unsatisfactory, have you
ever consulted a physician?" Not all of these questions should
be asked, nor will they all be necessary, but some of them will
hit the trail of the difficulty. All are legitimate questions, however, whose answers should reveal the trouble.

A girl came to me saying she was going to get a divorce,
that she and her husband had never been happy, although they
had two children together. I said, "Why did you get married?"
She replied, "I got married because my mother and father

quarreled all the time." I asked, "What about your life with your husband?" She said, "We have always quarreled." She talked on for some time describing their differences of opinion many of which had to do with their attitudes toward religion and social reform. The wife's description of her husband led me to believe he was a hard-working, conscientious, complacent young man who was trying to get along in his small community, while she wanted to change the world. I said, "What about your marital relations?" She answered, "We have none. He is impotent. He says I'm frigid. I don't want to have anything to do with him. I want a divorce but he has not wanted to give it to me because of the children." I said, "What do you want to do?" She said, "I want to be free to write. I'm sure I can write." I said, "So you have made your husband frigid so as to drive him to give you a divorce?" (a poor question).

A few months later she wrote, "Contrary to your advice I got a divorce. My ex-husband married his secretary two weeks later. I am very happy. The children are with me and I am spending my time writing." I had not told her she should not get a divorce; in fact I thought she should. I had pointed out some of the factors in the situation and she had not liked their looks. She had married to get away from home but she made the mistake of having children before she went on to the next step in her search for freedom.

A woman of fifty came for counseling concerning her marital situation. Her husband had repeatedly asked her for a divorce but would not take aggressive steps to secure one himself. The husband had failed in one position after another. The family lived frugally but their three daughters had all been educated, one of them had married. The wife questioned whether she should agree to her husband's request for a divorce —she suspected that he had gone with other women at various times. My questions to her were, "How much does your mar-

age really mean? What will happen to your husband in case
divorce is secured? How much do you care?" While she came
ɔ a clergyman for counsel because from a religious standpoint
ɪe believed divorce wrong, I did not challenge her along those
nes. Too often the church has been used to frustrate and
ɪppress spiritual growth through insisting that mismated
ɔuples remain married when they have never been able to
ɛach a union emotionally through their affection for each
ther.

A person who has reached fifty or fifty-five and has gone
hrough one failure after another is not apt to have courage
ɪough to break out of a marital situation which is also a
ailure. This wife needed to be helped to lessen the emotional
ressure which she had maintained upon her husband steadily.
'his is one of those situations where it is doubtful if permanent
ain can be made due to the age of the persons involved and
he long history of failure.

We may expect an increase in marital counseling in view of
ɪe new independence which the war has brought for women.
Vorld War I opened many fields of industry for women;
Vorld War II has opened an infinite number of others. No one
ɛriously expects women to leave these new fields of activity
ɪto which they have gone. This will mean economic independ-
ɪce so that the economic and moral double standard between
ɪen and women will increasingly disappear. While we may
xpect considerable difficulty in adjustment in the immediate
ɛars ahead, ultimately this new independence should mean
ɔiritual and moral gains, not during the period of adjustment,
ut eventually.

C. COUNSELING WITH YOUNG PEOPLE

There is more interest in counseling with young people than
ɪith any other group, and there is more work being done by

pastors in counseling with this group than with any other. Even so, pastors are not doing enough. The schools are doing an increasing amount of work in both vocational and therapeutic counseling but their programs are limited by the number of trained counselors who are available. For years the Young Men's and Young Women's Christian Association have carried on work of this nature with young people from a religious standpoint, which has been helpful in that their counselors have made up for lack of training through their genuine interest in the persons whom they attempted to help. In the large churches the pastors have usually delegated this important task to assistants which in some instances has been unfortunate.

A lad of seventeen told me of having gone to his pastor for help with a problem. He was in love but his mother did not like his sweetheart; the mother insisted that the boy sit with the family at church while he wanted to sit with the girl. When he suggested to his mother that the girl sit with his family his mother had become angry and said she would not have them sitting together as if they "were engaged." The boy's father said little. Finally the boy went to his pastor with his problem; the pastor listened to the story and then agreed to talk with the boy's father who was a member of his official board, but did not carry out his promise. In describing his pastor to me the boy said, "He laughs at us and kids us about the things we go to him with. To us they are serious even though they may not seem so to him. Several of my friends have tried to talk to him but he treats them all the same way. None of us will ever go back to him." Neither would I if he were my pastor.

Young people of high school age seek the pastor's help most frequently for vocational guidance. Even though they may be pretty well settled in the selection of their life work they are desirous of pastoral approval and encouragement. If they were encouraged to come by the pastor they would do so even more. In some mysterious sense his approval, like his blessing in marriage, seems like the approval of God. As the pastor moves among his young people he ought constantly to be asking them, "What are your plans for the future?" This carries him into a discussion of life work, preparation and schooling, and frequently of boy-girl problems and marriage because choosing a profession almost always involves delaying marriage past the time when the desire for marriage is strongest.

The Reverend Granger Westberg, now chaplain of Augustana Lutheran Hospital in Chicago, hit upon the plan of sending out cards to his Sunday school youngsters and young people inviting them to his study for conferences regularly every six months. He started with the seven-year-old youngsters in Sunday school and worked up through the young people in high school and then included his young adults. The first time they came they were apprehensive but he soon put them at ease by explaining he wanted to get better acquainted. The next time his card went out inviting them to come they came eagerly. His high school age students were most responsive of all to this interest, especially as he talked to them about their course of study and helped interpret it to them. This also gave him an opportunity to discuss their life-work plans. He got a one hundred per cent response in this program from his Sunday school group and his young people and approximately a ninety per cent response from students of his denomination in the local college. Few of these students were members of his church, but they welcomed his interest in them.

This program was launched with an announcement both from the pulpit and in the bulletin to the effect that cards would soon go out to the Sunday school students and young people inviting them to the pastor's study for an interview. The purpose of this program, he explained, was to enable the pastor to get better acquainted with the youngsters individually. Announcements were also made through the Sunday school and young people's society. Here is the card as Pastor Westberg sent it out:

Dear *George:*

Your pastor would like you to stop in at the church study for a friendly visit on *Wednesday, April 6, at 4:30 P. M.* If you happen to be with a friend at the time feel free to bring him or her with you. If you cannot come at the time indicated, kindly call telephone number 27 for a later appointment.

Sincerely,

GRANGER E. WESTBERG, Pastor

This card was mimeographed with italic portions written in. The reasons for this was that this form makes the impression that the call is impersonal in that every one is getting a similar card; also it is a time saver.

This program would seem to have great possibilities as a method of launching a significant counseling program. It can work in almost any situation except possibly the rural church. It has the advantage of being planned, orderly, and complete. Of course, no plan will work unless it is tried. The counselor must have personality and skill enough to take advantage of the opportunity once the young people are in his study, all of which comes under the head of the art of counseling.

When given the opportunity young people will want to discuss their choice of school and college. The pastor will need to know as much about special schools and courses of training as he can. For instance, many will never have heard about occupational therapy, or know that there are schools for the training of occupational therapists; neither will they have much idea about how to go about applying for acceptance to a school for specialized training. I am constantly amazed that top-notch young women, contemplating nursing, go to second- and third-rate training schools.

It is not that the average pastor will need to have information at his finger tips concerning vocations, schools and colleges, but he will know how to get information as it is needed while the young people and their parents will not. Many a youngster will receive little attention or encouragement from his parents as he attempts to make his plans. The pastor's interest in his future will be more important than the actual information which he gives. Selecting a life work and selecting a wife or husband are the two greatest decisions we make; naturally the pastor ought to be interested and helpful to his young people about them.

When the pastor has established contact with his young people and has shown his interest in them through inviting and keeping their confidences, they will come to him with their affairs of the heart, especially when those affairs become complicated. In the Reverend Mr. Westberg's plan the pastor knows of these affairs before they go badly and thus has the opportunity of being helpful before the people have become so seriously entangled that great suffering results. In counseling of this kind the pastor is helpful largely on the basis of what he can avoid doing. The church has been "against" so many things young people have wanted to do and have done, not because pastors have been blind but because the church is dominated by frustrated laymen who have failed in practically everything they have done, including their own family life. The clergy, therefore, cannot put into effect the kind of program they know young people need. Counseling which is done in a quiet, personal, inoffensive way can often offset the pastor's helplessness in other areas.

The mousy little girl who is not attractive and has every

chance of becoming a wall flower—that girl who, as a woman, will find her way to the psychiatric clinic or into the homes of her more fortunate neighbors to be a slave for their children while her heart yearns for children of her own—is one who will be on the pastor's list. She will come in fearfully when he sends for her; otherwise she will never dare to come. In facing such a girl the pastor has difficulty in deciding what his responsibility is. Theoretically he should assume the problem is one of retardation and try to be of assistance until he has exhausted all possibilities. Many girls, if they are helped to understand how to use what the Lord has given them, can develop personal charm so as to overcome their lack of natural attractiveness. The psychologist believes that the person who persists in making herself unattractive does so with a purpose, oftentimes to punish a parent who has failed to give her a feeling of security which is gained through love. The pastor will be helpless in overcoming such an attitude in view of the limited amount of time and the tremendous demands upon it, but sometimes he will be able to enlist the aid of someone else in a girl's behalf so that she will come to know what real affection is even though she does not have it at home.

Young people, facing temptation and suffering from guilt feelings, will come to the pastor to talk about the situations in which they find themselves, particularly in their social relations, as new horizons open for them in high school, college and business. There they see how others live and come into close contact with young people whose standards are different from their own. This has been true in the military service. A father showed me a letter from his son who had been wounded in the Cassino fighting. He wrote, "I have not taken a drink although the boys often invite me to drink with them and a bartender offered to give me a drink. The girls are easy here.

I wait outside the house until the others come out. I did not do those things at home and I will not do them here." Our hearts go out to that boy in the rugged loneliness of his determination to follow the ideals of his youth. He added, "You may pass this on to M (his sweetheart), as I don't know how to write it to her."

Not all young people will have that boy's will power and ultimately they find their way to the pastor with feelings of guilt because they blame themselves for having been weak and think of themselves as unworthy of the affection of a lovely girl. It then becomes the minister's task to put them back on their feet so that they will be able to go on; their future need not be ruined by a lone episode. Life is not ruined except as we permit it to be. The pastor is the one who will see these experiences for what they are and will help re-establish a young man or young woman's self-respect through his ability to "see life steadily and see it whole." Through his perspective he will calmly listen to the story, taking plenty of time, letting the confession work itself through, being neither over-eager with reassurance nor curious as to details of the experience. Many young people will feel they must tell their beloved of their experience and break off their engagement. The pastor would be wise to allow adequate time for counsel, pointing out that there is no hurry. While a few days will not alter the facts of the situation they may help a person to see the whole experience more calmly. I usually say, "I want to have a little time to go over this in my mind and then I want to see you again." If the youngster is quite emotional I make it the next day; if he seems relieved by our talk I make an appointment for two days later or even longer. In each instance I say, "If I were you I would not talk to anyone else just yet. We'll decide later about what you are to tell Mary." His willingness to tell his sweetheart the story is sufficient and there is no need to carry the story further to cause her suffering and raise doubts in her mind which she might not be able to handle.

The war has brought many young people to the pastor to discuss the problem of conscientious objection to war. Many pastors have not been helpful counselors upon this question because they are not disciplined to be objective; their own feelings enter into the counseling experience and ruin their chance of helping a person make up his own mind. After all, the counselees are the ones who will suffer criticism, social isolation, pangs of guilt, physical pain or death, as the case might be, not the pastor, and it is his obligation to hear their stories out and help in whatever way he can.

Young people come to the pastor with problems of belief as they begin to broaden their understanding of the universe through the study of science and other subjects in school, and they seek reassurance from the pastor. Again, his help will turn upon his objectivity and the kind of understanding of his work and his God which he has achieved. These opportunities afford him excellent teaching opportunities as well as counseling responsibility.

Counseling with young people, the youngsters of the early grades as well as high school and young adult age, calls for constant alertness on the part of the pastor to make opportunities for such contacts and to follow up the contacts as they present themselves. The pastor who is too busy to spend some time upon picnics, hikes, parties and banquets with his young people is skipping a vital part of his pastoral responsibility; if they fail to seek his counsel he had better examine his ministry and rebudget his time.

D. COUNSELING WITH ADULTS

My first thought was to write about counseling with parents in this section, but I realize that there are those who come to the pastor who are not parents or, if parents, the fact is of secondary importance to the problems they wish to discuss. Adults will seek the pastor's help for various reasons, but regardless of the presenting story the basic problems will be those discussed in chapter VIII. Therefore, I will point out only a few general observations here that have to do with counseling with adults.

Such counseling will grow out of routine calling, and from ideas that are gained from the pastor through his preaching concerning personal problems as discussed later in chapter XV. Because of the growing popularity of counseling and in view of the men and women in the military service who are receiving help from the chaplains through counseling, it may be that the average layman will come to realize that the pastor can be of help to him as he faces personal crises. As our clergy become trained for this important task we will be able to carry on an educational program for the church at large to that effect. Setting up office hours is not enough, but office hours for the Protestant clergy will be necessary as counseling becomes popular, just as regular hours for confession are held by the Roman Catholic clergy. If the program of counseling with young people initiated by Granger Westberg, which is discussed in the preceding section, comes into general practice, these youngsters, upon becoming adults, will come naturally to their pastor for personal counseling.

Here is a list of the problems with which adults have come to me most frequently. Naturally our discussion will overlap with that discussed under routine calling, for the same type of problems may come to the pastor's attention whether he is the aggressor or whether the parishioner seeks his help. In the latter instance our work is easier for we have a different type of authority with the one seeking help, for the parishioner recognizes he needs assistance even though he may be unwilling to follow through so as to actually achieve it.

1. Parishioners come to the pastor seeking employment. Sometimes work is actually what is desired and needed, and sometimes it is the excuse a parishioner will make for coming to him to discuss something else. The pastor will do well to follow the rule of taking time and inquiring into the general spiritual condition of the parishioner. "How are things going?" "Why are you quitting your present job?" "Where have you worked?" "How is your family?" "What would you like most to do?" Any of these questions will open up the larger areas of a person's spiritual condition.

In dealing with need for employment the pastor should have business contacts and especially contacts with employment agencies to which he can send people. This should be a personal contact, not just a name in the telephone book, so that he can make whatever personal interpretation is necessary. The person who does not need some special boost or help will find his own employment. In smaller communities such requests are not apt to come to the minister.

2. Another will be the person seeking relief. This request is becoming unusual in that public relief is well organized and knowledge of relief agencies are so well known that our people make their own contacts directly. There will be occasions when supplementary relief is needed, which will come to the attention of the pastor either directly or through other parishioners. The pastor should have some funds available for such use; many churches make provision for such funds through special contributions made at communion services.

Special mention should be made concerning the person, usually a man, who comes to the pastor with a story, frequently on Sunday when the agencies are closed, and asks for two dollars or five dollars, to buy food or a railroad ticket, or shoes, or something. It is surprising how even the sophisticated pastors of large city churches fall for these "touches." A good rule is never to give out cash; all you need to do is to offer to buy the food that is asked for, or offer to call an agency where a "friend" of yours works, and your desperately needy person vanishes. If this seems a little cold-blooded to you take the trouble to spend time with a social worker and learn something about panhandlers and professional bums.

3. There are many who come seeking advice concerning a physician, simply because they do not know whom to call. Others will come because they are displeased with the medical care they are receiving and some will have a just complaint. The best procedure is to direct the parishioner to a good general practitioner rather than to a specialist; the specialist will be recommended by the general practitioner if one is needed. Exception to this is the obstetrician or the pediatrician, whom the pastor may recommend directly. Many communities will have only general practitioners, who do everything, including surgery. The doctor who never refers some surgery on to the great medical centers is one who may be looked upon as a poor diagnostician.

4. Parishioners will seek counsel concerning their mother or father, and sometimes both. This is apt to turn upon the question of what to do about mother now that father has died, as she has no place to go. Sister cannot take care of her and husband does not think she should live with them because of the children. This is a real problem and one that can make for difficulty. Elderly people are sensitive about being pushed off somewhere but plans usually can be made that are satisfactory to all. Sometimes the problem is simply that the daughter feels

guilty because mother cannot live with her and needs reassurance from the pastor to the effect that mother should not live with her. In other generations when houses were large and when there was work for all, especially upon the farm, this was no problem, but in the city where people live in small houses and apartments and where there is less work it is a difficult situation. The pastor needs to be fairly passive in his role but he can reassure a sensitive parishioner. On occasion he may even need to be positive in his support of the son-in-law's wishes who feels that mother cannot live with them. At the same time he can seek information concerning possible homes where elderly people can live comfortably. Old age pensions are causing many elderly persons to receive a welcome they did not have before.

5. Couples desiring to adopt a child should be referred to a good child-placing agency. Sometimes it is a matter of going to more than one. State adoption laws vary; there are still some where such agencies exist for an economic purpose. Any agency, where there is a fee for the adoption of a baby and where little investigation is made of the prospective parents, is to be avoided. Again, it is a matter of securing information from a reliable social worker concerning child-placing agencies in a given community or recommending one elsewhere. Many agencies will give preference to a couple who come recommended by a pastor, if the pastor is known and his judgment trusted. He should be certain that the couple seeking a child can give it love and emotional security. Many girls can have babies of their own with proper medical attention. It is desirable for the pastor to make some inquiry as to why a couple desires to adopt a baby rather than have one of their own.

6. Parishioners often come to the pastor seeking help about a son or daughter who is having what they think is an unfortunate courtship which they fear will lead to a bad mar-

riage. The parents are usually right but the situation is complicated by many factors. It is important to get the story as clearly as possible, being concerned particularly with the parents' attitude. In this problem we are of most assistance in trying to help parents keep the door open; parents seldom want to lay down an ultimatum but feel they are forced to. I have said to parents, "Suppose they get married and their marriage fails; what will your attitude be?" Again, "Can you discuss the problem calmly with Mildred, or Jack?" Sometimes we are asked to try to break up an attachment and we should be willing to talk with the youngster and get his point of view. To take sides in such a dispute is questionable even though we agree strongly with one or the other. The boy or girl who asks our opinion seriously about a prospective wife or husband is in doubt. Our answer may be, "Why do you ask me?" thus giving the doubts an opportunity to come out into the open for examination. We should not make the decisions; we should help to clarify the issues and bring some reason into confused situations.

7. Parishioners will come to the pastor to discuss church problems and programs. Some few of them will concern the pastor's work directly in that they will have to do with a decision he has made, a program he desires, a sermon he has preached. If so, it is apt not to be a counseling situation. Often it will have to do with the church school, the women's society, the official board, the church building or the budget. Sometimes the conference deals with the parishioner's difficulties—it may be a church school teacher who is having difficulty with a youngster and desires help, or a member of the women's society who was due to be elected president but was not. Perhaps it is a member of the choir who is not permitted to sing solos, or a member of the board who does not like a decision that was made. These and many other problems come to the pastor under

the head of church program but actually turn upon personality problems. The pastor's method is the same with practically all: listening, interpretation, reassurance, sometimes referral to someone else; all of which takes time and mental discipline.

8. Another problem that presents itself frequently is that of a wife who is concerned because her husband is drinking. If it is a case of heavy drinking, of true alcoholism, which is characterized by an uncontrolled drinking appetite where the individual drinks himself into unconsciousness with no ability to stop once he has started, the minister should suggest medical treatment. The results are not encouraging in such cases even with medical treatment. "Alcoholics Anonymous" is an organization comprised of former alcoholics who are having fairly good results with this problem; their organization is spreading steadily although as yet it is confined to the larger cities. Information may be gained about their organization by writing to Post Office Box 658, New York (8), New York.

If it is a case of social drinking that your parishioner describes, with some question in her mind about "other women," it is well to encourage her to tell you as much as she will about their marital life, including why they were attracted to each other and why they became married. Finally, it is well to inquire into the nature of their sexual adjustment; if this is unsatisfactory then referral to a physician for examination and sex counsel is in order. Mismarriage is one of the great causes of drinking and the pastor cannot be helpful by attacking the problem of drink directly, neither does he need to counsel immediately with the husband, although this may be desirable eventually. If the husband refuses to cooperate and gives no intimation that he desires to change his behavior, then it is safe to assume that he is attempting to break up his marriage by his behavior and the wife should be helped to see that fact and accept it, for it takes two people to make a successful marriage.

9. The problem of homo-sexuality is another that will come to the pastor occasionally, so that he needs some understanding of it. Our society does not recognize that a third sex exists and we make no provision for such a fact in our thinking. Authorities, what few there are, differ upon the causes of homo-sexuality. They do agree, however, that the chances are slight of helping a person who is strongly attracted toward members of his own sex to make a hetero-sexual adjustment. Such a person should be referred to a psychiatrist for counsel; if none is available in your community send him to a city where one is available. Do not waste time and run risks so far as your own reputation is concerned in dealing with something you know nothing about. There are no exceptions in dealing with this problem. It just is not the pastor's problem.

A number of these persons are attracted into the ministry and some few are ordained before their tendencies become strong; some even marry and have children. Eventually their ministries are terminated, but not often without some unfortunate circumstances. As more adequate counseling facilities are made available in the theological seminaries these individuals should be spotted and directed out of the ministry into other types of work. Many are talented and have contributions to make to society. They cannot make them by becoming ministers, however, and none should be encouraged to try to work out their adjustments in this profession.

10. Marital counseling has already been discussed in a preceding section as a major problem that comes to the pastor.

11. Frequently elderly people will find their way to the pastor's office, particularly if he encourages them to come. They come with various requests, sometimes with complaints or

criticism but their basic problem is loneliness and boredom. These conferences take time and they are discouraging for the pastor in that little permanent gain can be made, and yet he cannot close his door to such persons. In view of the tremendous, largely untouched, problem of loneliness among elderly persons it is surprising how few do call the pastor or seek attention for themselves.

Counseling with adults has always been interesting to me because one hits problems with teeth in them more frequently than in counseling with young people, although there is deep soul-satisfaction in seeing youngsters develop and blossom out with help and encouragement. There is no such thing as a problem that is insignificant either among young people or adults; all are serious from the standpoint of the counselee, and it is from that standpoint that we must work.

CHAPTER VII

WAR-TIME COUNSELING

A. MEN GOING INTO THE SERVICE

WHILE the great recruiting and training phase of the war is over, so that the pastor's opportunity for counseling with men and women going into the service is past, there are many who are still being called and recruiting will continue until the war's end. Even after the end of hostilities we may expect men, particularly of the younger ages, to continue to be drafted as replacements for those serving in occupied countries; we may also expect a military training program in the future years such as America has never known in the past. Therefore, it is opportune for the church and the clergy to be examining their future counseling service for these young people, even though they have done little of it for those who have already gone. Those who are being called now need this service more than those who were called earlier.

The Westberg Plan, described in the preceding chapter, if put into general usage, is the kind of plan that eventually will meet this need. If our young people are accustomed to coming regularly to the pastor for counseling they will come naturally and easily before they leave for military induction. If they have not been accustomed to coming they will appreciate a call from the pastor, in light of the experience they are facing. They will want to talk to him about many things; some will not have bothered to join the church although they may be active in the young people's department. Two fine young men who attended our church regularly but were not members requested that I baptize them before they left for camp; had it not been for the crisis of going away for military service they probably would have neglected this vital affiliation for years.

If the pastor affords the opportunity, the boys will want to talk about their girl friends, often desiring his help in reaching a decision about marriage plans. This may involve another conference with both the girl and the boy, or with his parents. Also, the subject of vocation following military service will come up for discussion. They may seek advice as to the branch of the service they should choose which will fit them for a vocation, although most men will have this question pretty well decided before the time of their leaving arrives. Many of those applying for Officers Candidate School will use the minister's name as a reference.

One of the subjects which the pastor should bring up in these discussions is the fact that a chaplain, a representative of the church, regardless of his particular denominational affiliation, will be in the camp to which they are going. He should suggest that the chaplain does counseling and that he is a person to get acquainted with; further, that it would be interesting to have news from his parishioner concerning the religious services in the camp or on board ship. Some pastors have written post chaplains to the effect that such and such a person has recently come to his camp. Whenever possible the lad's outfit should be included in the letter which saves the chaplain time in looking up this information. Thus he is able to call a man in and say, "Your pastor wrote me you were here."

Secondly, the pastor should give a New Testament to each of his parishioners going into the service. It is unfortunate that so many pastors have overlooked this opportunity, so that our men and women have had to secure their New Testaments from other sources than their home churches.

Third, the pastor should say to each young man and woman that he will be writing regularly to them and that others in the church may write from time to time. I am assuming that the pastor will keep his word and will write every month or six weeks to his parishioners who are in the armed services. A medical officer told me, "My minister is the only one, aside from my family and a few friends, who has remembered I am away from home. Before I came into the Army I took my church for granted, but I gave a lot of time and money to the Community Chest and other organizations. No one else has so much as written me a note saying, 'We miss you. Good luck.' When I get out of the Army the church will come first and these other organizations will get what's left." The same thing will be true in reverse if others have remembered the servicemen who are away but the church has forgotten.

Finally, the pre-induction counseling conference should close with a prayer. This prayer should be as personal and as significant as the pastor can make it. At a later time he may want to send a copy of this prayer to his parishioner.

To be able to make this conference significant and to include all that needs to be covered the pastor will want to have from forty-five minutes to an hour with each person and he will want to see him alone. There are few young people who would not appreciate and long remember such a conference. The tragedy of the clergyman's work during the early phases of our training program was that so few ministers carried out a plan as outlined above; even now it is not too late to start, however.

B. The Families of Service Men

Many of our pastors have become concerned about post-war planning and the new world, but have failed to keep in close touch with the families of the men in service, particularly with those whose sons and husbands are in combat theatres of the war.

The problems of the family are largely two-fold: apprehension concerning the physical safety of the service man, and loneliness. There are not many instances of suffering because of physical needs nor do guilt feelings crop up often among members of the family. A few instances of guilt feelings find their way to the pastor, usually in the girl who has fallen in love with another chap although she is engaged to a service man. Even this problem rests back upon loneliness.

Some of our people have literally worn themselves out through worrying about their loved ones. The pastor's call, attention, reassurance and prayer will do much to break the clasp of this apprehension. We have all known mothers and fathers, wives and sweethearts who started going to pieces emotionally even before a boy went off to camp. This can be said in general, as it is said of the service men who crack up emotionally; those who were already emotionally unstable are the ones who have trouble. That does not change the pastor's opportunity nor alter his responsibility, however.

When I rang the doorbell of a home which had received word a few hours before that an aviator son was missing, I was greeted by the mother with these words, "This makes it very real." Later she apologized for her remark which she felt was ungracious, but which I felt was perfectly natural. Of course the minister's call made her fear more real, but suppose I had not called? Suppose I had not had a part in that family's daily apprehension, watchfulness, loneliness and prayers? They would have felt their church had deserted them and that God did not suffer with them.

One of the things that has made the chaplain's work effective is that he is there with the men, working, marching, praying, suffering, dying with them. That makes God real! The chaplain's opportunity has been great not because of his preaching but because of his presence. So in our presence with those who are afraid for sons and husbands and brothers and fathers who are in places of danger. The chaplain is there in danger with them, while the civilian clergyman at home is with those who watch and pray and wait.

The problem of the chronic worrier is a deep-seated difficulty, usually gained through early parental conditioning. To say to such a person, "Don't worry," is like trying to check a hurricane wind by whistling into it. The mother who has not let her son grow up but finds him called into the military service will have a hard time, for such a person is emotionally starved herself. Many such mothers are either widows or are separated from their husbands so that their love has become centered in the boy. Once he is in the service he may make a desperate effort to break away from mother's apron strings. In this he should be encouraged. The pastor who has done a thorough job of his pre-induction counseling will discover these problems, if he has not identified them before. He should call regularly upon such a mother; or better, urge her to come to him for counsel. The results will be better with this problem if she makes the effort which coming to the pastor's study involves. While the obvious fact of her emotional dependence upon her son must not be pointed out, through asking questions about the way she has reared him, her indulgence and her relations with him, she can be led to make the discovery herself.

This same problem is faced by the pastor in counseling with parents, particularly with mothers, who object to their sons getting married. The problem is more acute in war time due to hurried courtships and quick marriages. The young people feel they work against time; theirs is "so little time" as a popular novel of 1943 expresses it. If it is a question of a marriage which has been planned for some time but the war makes it urgent that they speed up their plans, in general I encourage them to go ahead and get married. The marriage stabilizes both of them.

In the case of a mother who has tied her son closely to her and he breaks away and gets married in spite of her we may expect severe reactions from the mother. Since it is a matter of getting married *to spite* mother, the boy is seldom fortunate or wise in his choice of a wife. A mother went with her son's fiancée to a military camp to visit him. Both were entertained in the camp guest-house. The son paid so much attention to the girl that the mother went home indignantly the second day, writing back to the company commander that the guest-house rules should be more strict, since her son had spent the night with his girl friend there. This was not true. The mother's action so enraged the son that he was determined to marry the girl immediately to spite his mother; only through talking with his chaplain did he overcome his resentment and avoid a hasty marriage.

Another vital problem is the pastor's ministry to the bereaved in war time. I feel that our ministers are and will continue to do fairly effective work with the families of the men and women who are killed in military service. Some have been uncertain as to what kind of a religious service to have or whether to have any at all. The best practice seems to be to hold a memorial service as each notice is received; such a service helps to release tensions within the family, thus enabling them to accept the fact of the death. The problem is more difficult with those reported missing; many of the missing will return and the families know this. At the same time there are many who will not return, and families know this also. Think of those lost in sea actions! The Navy chaplain who was aboard the aircraft carrier, *Yorktown,* when she was lost told me of the inquiries from families which poured into his office when news was released of the carrier's loss. These inquiries sought all kinds of information about the nature of the battle and whether a son was lost through drowning or battle wounds. It was impossible to answer these questions but we can see why they would arise.

The families of men who are wounded live under considerable stress but the Red Cross and the chaplains are doing much to relieve this apprehension. Naturally, many cannot be helped because the number is so great and because in many instances the news is not reassuring. The pastor's attention, and especially his prayers, are important in the face of this problem. The need for women in industry and in the various phases of Red Cross work has helped. The U. S. O. has also been a great help in relieving apprehension. The U. S. O. volunteer program, particularly, is carried largely by the families of service men. The U. S. O. was slow in finding jobs for fathers but now even they are carrying a significant load.

The reason that the mental health of our nation in general is so much better in war time than it was during the deep depression is that during a war there is work for all, and more. Every person is important, every person's work is needed, while in the depression our people were turned away "unwanted and unneeded." William James once said, "If you want to punish a person, ignore him."

C. The Psychoneurotic

For the first time in the military history of the United States men and women are being dismissed from the service with the diagnosis of psychoneurosis. They are being dismissed at the rate of about ten thousand a month which means that some are returning to every community. Obviously many of those who are receiving the diagnosis of psychoneurosis have little wrong with them; we have so few psychiatrists that careful medical studies cannot be made. It is difficult for even a skilled psychiatrist to distinguish between a person who is emotionally unstable, one who has a definite organic but obscure disease, and one who is a malingerer, who is deliberately trying to get out of the service. Medical military authorities recognize that the psychoneurotic diagnosis has been overdone but the problem is so difficult and time so vital that the man or woman who wants to get out of the service can do so because the physician cannot distinguish between the really sick person and the one who is not. In the light of our cultural background of a free democracy, especially in view of the fact that the government has recognized the conscientious objector and given him a free choice which excuses him from military service, a man who complains of pain but where no condition of pain can be found, is dismissed from the service. From the psychiatric point of view any man or woman who wants to be released from the present military conflict, regardless of the reasons aside from religious grounds, is definitely sick and should be dismissed for the good of those who must carry the load. Morale and effective military operations are carried on by a group of persons working together to achieve a given end; the person who is unable or unwilling to do his part is judged abnormal, and rightly so. We recognize that in war time and in the military situation the so-called normal is different from the normal of peace time, and the person who is unable to shift to the norm of war is not of much help in the military service. "The soldier develops abnormal reactions which would be considered pathological in peace time," a commander of the Spanish Republican Army once said. "I think that during war everybody is upset, nervous, jittery, and perhaps slightly crazy. It is no wonder, then, that you do not find an increasing number of insane. You simply lack a normal background for comparison." [1]

Thus the psychoneurotic comes back to the community, sick from the standpoint of the military medical officer. He is confused in his own mind and misunderstood by his family and friends, because the public as a whole has simply never heard of the term, psychoneurosis, and understands little or nothing of its meaning. Most of the men receive some interpretation from the medical officers, some are able to understand it, others are not. The picture is confused because many early psychotic persons have been inducted into the service also. The crisis of the training experience pushed many of these cases along so that they are really ill when they return home and face the need of almost immediate hospitalization. One lad who came to my attention wandered off two weeks after his return home and we had to institute a search for him covering three states. He had returned with a definite diagnosis of early schizophrenia from his military psychiatrist but with no recommendation for treatment or hospitalization. His mother, being a religious fanatic herself, had interpreted his pronouncements and peculiar behavior as religious zeal and had taken no steps to help him until he wandered off.

Another lad with whom I talked had been under psychiatric treatment before his induction into the army. He had presented a letter from his psychiatrist to his draft board which stated clearly, "Under no circumstances should Blank be inducted into military service." Nevertheless the board called him; once called he failed to show the letter to his induction medical officer as he was anxious to do his part. Through luck in his assignment he was able to stay in the Army a year but considerable damage was done to his emotional stability during that

[1] *Psychiatry in War* by Emilio Mira, M. D., p. 12. W. W. Norton & Company, Inc., New York, 1943.

time. The shock of his dismissal was severe and he needed further treatment in order to stay out of a hospital.

These severe cases have confused the understanding of the public so that they are apt to think of the psychoneurotic person as an early psychotic, as a "queer" or as a "crazy" person. The result is that many men claim other reasons as the cause of their dismissal; flat feet or poor eye sight is understood and respected, while a mental condition is not.

Most of the psychoneurotic group need counseling, some of them need a great deal of very skilled counseling, but it is just not available. We do not have enough skilled workers—medical, psychological or otherwise. The pastor will have to carry a major part of this load, for poor as his training is, he still is better equipped in his understanding of people than is the layman.

The methods of counseling with the psychoneurotic are those described in Part Four, with a major emphasis upon *passive listening*. There is no great need to probe into the details of his experiences; if he wants to tell them well and good, if not pass them by. If he returns for further conferences, and he should be encouraged to, and if he talks around what he has done, or makes vague references to not understanding himself or his actions, he should be encouraged to tell more as he is suffering from a sense of guilt and desires reassurance. The psychoneurotic person should be reassured that he is not different from other people, that many people are unable to serve in the military machine and that the nation needs other workers, that he can make his contribution in another way, above all, that he is not insane. If he says he is "yellow" and lacks "guts" it might be pointed out to him that persons are put together emotionally in different ways.

I was introduced to a soldier who was waiting dismissal from the army as a psychoneurotic because he was a homo-sexual.

In civilian life he had been a dancer. I said, "Are you going to return to dancing when you get out?" He said, "No, not while the war is going on. There are other things that are more needed. I'm going to try to get a job in a war plant." The psychoneurotic should be encouraged to get a job and as vital and permanent a one as possible so that he may regain his self-respect and his confidence in himself. One such man tried to get two or three jobs but was turned down because he did not adequately explain his military status. He came to the conclusion that he was "snake-bitten" as he put it; then he began to drink. His father came to me in desperation saying the boy had "given up." I had one conference with him and got him a job within twenty-four hours. That was all that was needed to help him. Others will need more counseling and take more time.

D. THE RETURNING SERVICE MAN

Foremost among returning personnel are men and women on furlough, most of whom are home on leave from their training. Some are on their last leave before shipping to a theatre of combat, and there are others on furlough who have been in combat, many of whom will return to the fighting areas. The problems of men and women on furlough vary greatly; some suffer from feelings of guilt, discouragement and disillusionment. Others, particularly those facing combat, suffer feelings of apprehension, while still others dread returning to the loneliness of being separated from loved ones. This same feeling of loneliness crops up sometimes while the men are on leave; a feeling of loneliness in being separated from their military comrades. One soldier I knew, had been in the air corps eighteen months without leave; he was given a two-weeks furlough but returned to the service at the end of seven days, saying that after he had seen his family he was ready to return to work.

Early in the training program the military chaplains became realistic about the problem of the girl who claimed she was pregnant and insisted that the service man marry her. This realism might well have been passed on to our civilian clergy; even now it is well for us to see this problem clearly as we counsel with men returning from the service, many of whom will face the task of untangling marriages which should never have been made. Girls are much more cold-blooded about affairs of the heart, despite all their sentimentality, than men are. A girl falls in love pretty much when she wants to and *not* until she is ready to, while a man falls in love when a girl wants him to. The glamour of romance and all things pertaining thereunto are the skills of woman and she uses them as an artisan uses the skills which he has studied and mastered. Because of the way man is put together emotionally he is putty in the hands of a woman, while the opposite is not true, except in rare instances. Due to the speed and peculiar circumstances of the war situation girls have manipulated the service men to their desires as they pleased and few have realized it. When there had been an acquaintance and courtship before the war not many have been disturbed, but the short-time courtships have worried us all. The military authorities take the position of protecting the men; this is desirable from a military standpoint but it is also desirable from a moral standpoint in view of the above. The girl who gets pregnant does so pretty much because she desires to become pregnant for one reason or another; not always is it because she wants to get married, not always is it calculated and thought through by the girl.

One chaplain pointed out that ninety per cent of the girls who claimed they were pregnant were not at all. How many men went into marriage under the threat of exposure by the girl, we do not know, but the number is believed to be large.

We should remember this fact as we watch the divorce rate of the future and as we counsel with young people seeking help in unhappy marital situations. I do not place the whole blame upon women, in fact, I place blame nowhere. The girls were faced with the same loneliness the men faced and they chose to meet it in various ways. Far more faced it in other ways than did those of whom I have written above. As I traveled through the camps for the Y. M. C. A.—U. S. O. and watched hundreds of girls serving as hostesses in the clubs I marveled at their poise and good sense, and I was amazed at the little difficulty which had arisen so far as girls and boys were concerned in the U. S. O. clubs.

The problem of counseling with returning service men from the combat theatres, whether the men have been under fire or not, interests all of us. Approximately thirty per cent of the battle casualties in the armies of Britain and the United States are of an anxiety type. This has not been true of the Russian and German armies. No information is at present available on the figures in the Japanese army. Many of these anxiety casualties are being treated effectively near the front. Others who have gone through the difficult and soul-searing experiences of war will return home, never having been under medical observation or never having received psychiatric treatment. Some will be all right after they have gone through a "cooling off period" which may require but a few weeks, while for others it will be longer.

If your help is sought by the ex-serviceman the method should be that of passivity. In case the parishioner desires to talk, let him talk. Let him talk about anything he wants to talk about, and suggest he return for further talks. If his restlessness continues the pastor should suggest that help may be gained through talking about his experiences on what is called a catharsis basis—getting them out in the open. Some literally will thrust these experiences upon you, in which case little *reassurance* is needed.

The following is a record of such an experience as recorded by an Army chaplain.[2] Note the problems of fear, guilt and general terror. I inquired of the chaplain whether he thought his help was sought because the soldier was facing further combat and because he was worried about his wife. The chaplain replied that he thought both were active in causing the soldier to seek help. Such a story might come to any clergyman.

PRIVATE "B"

First Impression:

Private "B." was about 25 years of age, tall, dark complexion, black hair, slender build. His face was flushed and he seemed nervous. I recognized him as a recent replacement in the Regiment, released from a hospital where he had recovered from wounds received overseas.

First Interview:

"Hello! Come in," I said, as Private B. came to the office door. I turned to arrange a chair for him and asked him to sit down.

"Are you a Protestant chaplain?"

"Yes," I replied.

"I didn't know. I thought you might be a Catholic."

"There is a priest down at the next regiment if you would like to speak with a priest."

"Oh, no. I am Protestant. The chaplain in my former unit was a priest, so I guess I think of chaplains as priests. I was down a couple of times before tonight, but I didn't see anyone here then." He was nervous and appeared to be making conversation.

"There wasn't anyone here then. An officers' meeting was being held."

"You have to attend those too, do you, sir?"

[2] These notes are published with the permission of the War Department. They were written by Chaplain Arthur P. Colbourn.

"Oh, yes."

There was a pause. Private B. was finding it difficult to speak.

"You can see that I have been overseas." Apparently he noticed that I had observed the row of ribbons on his blouse. "I have just arrived at this camp from The Blank Army Hospital. Well, the thing is I don't seem to be able to take this life any more. My nerves are all shot." Here he stopped talking for a moment. "Here I am in a combat unit and expected to do full field duty, but I can only do limited duty. I was told at the hospital that I was to do only limited duty. Every time I put any pressure on this arm, I feel it all the way up to the shoulder. And the lower part of the arm and hand are numb. I can hardly feel anything, even carrying a rifle is difficult. Would you like to see what I am talking about? You could understand better."

"That might be a good idea." He showed me his arm and there were four scars in the muscle of his upper arm and a long incision scar from elbow to shoulder.

"Four 25-caliber went through my arm there. The long scar is the incision of the operation I had later. The nerve was affected and the doctor tried to fix it up."

"You got it across?" I continued.

"On Blank Island." He paused again. "I was out on patrol one night with eight men, I being a B & R gunner. I stumbled and fell so close to a group of Japs that they grabbed my gun away and I was left helpless. Luckily, my buddies got them with a grenade before they could finish me." Private B. was shaking noticeably now. "I suppose that the real trouble with me is that I am afraid." He put his head in his hands and sobbed openly for a moment. "I wasn't like this until now," he finally said between sobs. "Even after I got home on furlough upon being released from the hospital, I took it for granted I would return overseas. I even told my wife there was a two to one chance that I would. But this inspection taking place (special inspections were announced today which have been interpreted as a sign of overseas shipment soon), and it was announced by the captain that it was a fifty-fifty chance that we would not go on maneuvers in the spring, meaning that we were heading for overseas. I almost

went to pieces. Then tonight, I telephoned my wife in Blank. She i
going to have a baby. I couldn't get through to her at first. Ther
she told me she had been to the hospital today for a check-up. Every
thing is O. K. so far, but she has already had two miscarriages. Now i
when she needs me. God, I can't leave her now!" He began sobbing
again. "I guess I just can't take it any more. I can't bear the though
of going overseas." A pause. "Sir, I have done my part. Why not le
others go over and do the fighting now?"

"Nothing definite has come down about the division. I don't know
whether it will go over or not. It probably will in some capacity. W
didn't do very well in maneuvers so I don't know what's in store fo
us as a combat division," I added.

"You may not think it combat caliber. I know it isn't. But my old
division was a broom-stick set-up too, and it went over a few month
after Pearl Harbor. We couldn't believe it ourselves but we soor
began waking up. After weeks, we found ourselves at Blank whicl
the Marines and Army had taken a little while before. Then to Blank
Island where the Japs bombed and straffed us for fifty days straight
Then came the whole Blank Island campaign, thirty-eight days sleep
ing in fox-holes, eighteen of them in holes full of water because of the
constant downpour. Little or nothing to eat and always afraid to
move. We got used to living in the jungle itself after a while, bu
the Japs were always so sly. At night they would creep up and give
commands in English, thereby getting us mixed up, and then killing
all in sight. We soon got on to that trick! And then my company
got cut off from the rest of the battalion and was surrounded fo
thirty-six hours, and almost surrounded for several days more. It wa
bad enough during the day but at night it was ungodly!!! They
made the weirdest noises to add to the already weird noises of the
jungle. And you could hardly see a few feet ahead of you. You had
to keep a constant watch, never sleeping. The Japs were always in
filtrating at night, crawling quietly up to our fox-holes on thei
bellies, like snakes. They killed a number of my buddies that way
and you didn't sleep because you knew that was what would happer
to you. Twice I found buddies dead in the hole next to me, killed
that way." I saw his facial muscles stiffen and he stood up, his fac

turned pale. "One night I heard a noise and saw a Jap crawling about three yards from my fox-hole. I remained silent until he got within reach and then I got him with my knife. When I came to myself, I realized I had gotten out of the hole and cut his head completely off, and there he was in front of me bleeding to death." His face grew paler, and a look of utter anguish pervaded his whole countenance. "Chaplain, that wasn't human. I was a beast. I wasn't raised to do that. A man can't stand it! Oh God, a man can't stand it!" He sat down and sobbed again. "I guess I would have caved in altogether if another buddy hadn't been killed. Then I got mad again.

"We entered battle with one hundred eighty-seven in the company, and came out with ten. We got out only by having other companies come towards us and by making a desperate charge across a little valley and cleaning out a hillside." His face was now uplifted, almost as if in a trance. "I'll never forget that day. We were driven to desperation. There was nothing else to do but charge, and then the break-through! I'll never forget! I'll never forget!" The trance-like expression left him and he began talking slowly, more thoughtfully. "We had to seek 'em out because they were camouflaged so well, like wild animals hiding in the grass. There I was and everything was the very opposite from all I had been taught to expect in life. It seemed like some ungodly nightmare, yet I knew it was real.

"Our chaplain was there with us. He was right there, and with nothing to protect himself. Naturally we did all we could to protect him, but that wasn't much. He was wounded. I had to help bury him later. A brave man! My, he was a brave man!"

At this point he became conscious of my presence. Before, he was unburdening himself, almost unconscious of my being there, often talking rapidly and sometimes in a semi-trance condition. He settled back in his chair and said, with an embarrassed look—"I'm sorry. I shouldn't have gone on like this, and I know how busy you are." He glanced toward a letter I was writing when he came in.

"No, I was just writing a letter," I stated. "I'm glad you came in. It does one good to talk things over with someone. I often do."

"I think perhaps you're right."

"It relieves us of some of the tension and often our problems are a little clearer afterwards. I think it is a very healthy thing to do."

"Well, I feel better about it now, but I am sorry I came here the way I did. I had been drinking beer down at the P. X. I probably smelled pretty bad."

"You must have kept your breath to yourself. I am not going to condemn you for drinking it. You must form your own opinion about that. If you think it's wrong you shouldn't do it, but since I've been in the army I have become firmly convinced that it is better to have the P. X.s (Post Exchanges) sell beer here on the post than have the men going outside the camp and drinking hard liquor."

His face lightened a bit. "You're the first chaplain I ever heard talk that way, but I really think you're right."

There was a rap on the door—another soldier coming to see me. Private B. looked at me and asked—"What do you think can be done?"

"I don't know offhand. I am well acquainted with your company commander. Why don't I have a talk with him in view of your trouble with your arm, and your difficulty in doing full field duty?"

"That might get him down on me. I don't want to give the impression that I'm not able to take it."

"I don't think Captain S. would hold it against you. But it might be just as well not to say anything to him. I might check with the medicos and see what they have on your record. Then we can have a better idea what to expect—limited duty or full field."

"That would be a fine idea," he added. "I'll go along now. There is someone else to see you, but I feel a lot better."

"I'll check with the doctor tomorrow."

"I'll see you tomorrow night."

Second Interview: (Next night)

A rap was heard at the door almost as soon as I reached the office after dinner. "Come in," I said.

"I didn't mean to come quite so early, but I wanted to tell you how much better I feel. I was so stirred up last night that I was all mixed up. I just had to let off steam to somebody. I still don't know what I'll do if I have to go back overseas (here, tears came to his eyes) but I can do my best. That's all I can do."

"That's all any of us can do," I added.

"The shock of the announcement about going overseas is over a bit tonight, and I feel more in control of myself." There was a pause. "I am sorry I came in the way I did last night."

"No harm was done."

"I'm glad you take that attitude. It makes it easier to talk to you." There was a pause.

I said, "I haven't found out anything definite yet. I spoke to Dr. R. but he doesn't seem to have much of a record on you. He wants to examine you himself. The personnel office probably has your record, I can check there. Also, I don't know about the plans for the division. Our information is only by implication, but I have been told by the doctor that if we go overseas, those unfit for foreign service will be rejected at the port of embarkation."

"Yes, that's how it's done. We did that before," he answered. "I'll just have to make the best of it in the meantime. I suppose I've had it lucky. I feel that way much of the time, but not when I talk with many civilians. Many still think the Jap is a midget. They make me so mad, sir! Sometimes I have all I can do to control myself when I'm around them, especially when I think of my buddies still fighting over there. But I don't want to give the impression I dislike my country or its people. Many are sacrificing and doing a swell job. And none a better job than the air corps. I can never forget what they did for us at Blank Island. My unit landed first at Blank Island, with little opposition. But then we got a terrific pounding by Jap planes for about twenty minutes. Nevertheless, we had to set out right then for a beach near Blank on Blank Island, a distance of five miles, in open boats. It was awful watching those planes do their work, and we had only rifles and machine guns. But when we were about half way over, our chaps arrived from Blank Field on Blank. Oh! how they shot those Jap planes to pieces!! It was like having a death sentence commuted for us. How those fellows could fly and fight. And those Corsair planes were such beautiful things. I don't think I was ever so proud before of being an American. When we almost reached shore, all was still quiet on the land and we thought this strange. But just when we were about to step ashore, the Japs let loose with everything. They had been waiting for us in the jungles. . . . You see, I keep going on and on. But you get so full of the sights and smells that you see and smell them at work, at mess, and have nightmares while you try to sleep. At night especially, you often think you are back there in it. Sometimes you just think you can't stand it any longer."

"Did you ever try writing out your thoughts and impressions when you feel that way? Writing and talking with a trustful friend often relieves a lot of tension."

"I've never tried writing, but I certainly have been helped by talking things over here. It surely made things easier last night."

He rose to leave. There had been a rap at the office door. I remarked, "I have just received SPECIAL ORDERS to report to another camp. Chaplain Blank will remain here to continue with the work of the chapel. I hope you'll get acquainted with him. He'll be able to find out some more things for you concerning your status. I have to leave tomorrow."

"Will you be at the service tomorrow, sir?"

"Yes."

"Well, I'll be on hand. Thanks again. I'll see you tomorrow."

Next Morning: (Sunday)

Private B. was at morning worship. After the service he shook hands with me at the door. "One of the fellows has just told me that you are going overseas. Good luck, sir! I guess that's all I can say except that I wish you were staying with us here."

PART THREE

CONDITIONS OF EFFECTIVE
PASTORAL WORK AND COUNSELING

CHAPTER VIII

THE PERSONAL CRISIS

IN ONE sense the study of the personal crisis in an effort to understand spiritual needs is a negative approach. As clergymen and religionists we run the danger of becoming abnormally interested in people with problems. In this respect we may limit our work by becoming content with the relief of suffering and give little attention to the prevention of suffering, as is true of most physicians. Preventive medicine lags behind curative medicine because the latter is more interesting and dramatic. The intimate and satisfying personal relation between patient and physician is far more interesting than the emotional relationship between a man and a mosquito swamp. Fortunately there are a few who prefer the latter.

Because the person who is suffering needs what we have, we naturally are attracted to him. This is as it should be, but we must not be content in giving attention only to people with problems. The person who is not suffering has affection and faith already but needs to share them with those who need help. Some refuse to carry their part of this load and it becomes the pastor's task to enlist their interest; all too often he fails in this task. Psychology will eventually teach us why.

A basic principle in pastoral work is the recognition that life is a shifting, developing, regressing, growing experience. One thing in human nature we can be certain of is that people are different from each other and that a person is different from his former self at one time as judged against another. Different ideas, different moods, different interests, hopes, apprehensions, and loyalties claim his attention from time to time. The pastor must be capable of recognizing these various conditions and adapt himself to them. We must start with the parishioner where *he is*, not where we are. Since so much of our lives are lived against the background of suffering, in fact since creation comes out of suffering, we must give attention to the suffering experience. The personal crisis gives the clergyman his reason and opportunity for doing pastoral work. Without suffering we would not have religion, the church, or much of life as we know it. Suffering seems to be deep in the heart of the universe.

Religion had its rise in man's effort to establish a satisfactory and satisfying relationship with the world in which he lived. In primitive religion man sought to overcome suffering and the forces which threatened to destroy him; modern man does the same. It is late in the history of religion that man is religious because he gains satisfaction through being religious, when love of God displaces fear of God. Only out of suffering is deep love born.[1]

We can observe suffering as the primary moving force behind creation. At the same time we see suffering which is destructive, which fails. We must not make the mistake of glorifying suffering, lest it become an end in and of itself, but we take courage from the fact that good may come out of it. Without that belief and without the support of that knowledge it is doubtful if many of us would long remain pastors. We would be like unarmed children going out to battle against giants.

There are four types of suffering and, I believe, only four: pain, fear, guilt feelings, and loneliness. Some observers list

[1] For an excellent treatment of the whole subject of suffering see *Victorious Suffering* by Glover. $1.00. Abingdon-Cokesbury Press, Nashville and New York, 1942.

apprehension, worry, resentment and anger as additional types. The difference between apprehension and fear is only one of degree, and both may stem from guilt feelings. Resentment and anger stem from fear. We do not feel resentment and we do not become angry until we have been hurt physically or mentally, or until we face the danger of being hurt. The emotion of fear is different chemically from anger, but fear sets off anger. Therefore anger and fear should be studied and treated as one emotion.

These four emotions are the foundation stones of human behavior; the whole of life has to do with them. The struggle to avoid suffering accounts for our industrial, social, economic, recreational and religious life, and for our heroism in searching for new ways of life and living. To be sure, these four emotions are mixed up together, so that seldom do we deal with one apart from another, and then not for long.

A. Pain

Physical pain is the pure emotion; all others seem to have some relation to it in one way or another. It may be brought about by hunger, thirst, exposure, injury or disease. The severity of pain varies depending upon its cause; the pain brought about by angina pectoris is reported to be one of the most severe, while a person may have a leg severed and feel little pain at the time.

Pain has its positive values: without it we would not stir ourselves to work to secure the basic necessities of life, nor would we have developed powers of observing and harnessing the productivity of nature; without pain we should fall prey to the various kinds of injury and disease. Pain is basic and primitive in our natures; we hold it in common with other creatures of the animal kingdom.

Our lives are made up of little pains and we take them in our stride as the child learning to walk takes bumps and tumbles but gets up and tries again. But prolonged physical suffering we do not handle so well. Intellectually, emotionally and spiritually we lose our perspective; our confidence in our world goes to pieces. Our reasoning powers are the first to break under the pressure of prolonged suffering, but we have the power of observation which leads us to search for the cause of suffering even in the midst of it and for ways of gaining relief. Then we are close to the rise of primitive religion, for primitive man personalized everything around him. It will be a triumphant day when we dismiss the thought that our physical suffering is brought about by evil spirits or comes to us as punishment.

Pain needs to be listed with other emotions as a symptom for spiritual need only because we have been taught through the Hebrew and Christian religions that God will do all things for us if we pray hard enough. In that teaching there has been no recognition of time: that relief from suffering takes time, often a great deal of time, and even then the forces of nature and man may fail in gaining that relief. Further, our religious teaching has not pointed out clearly enough the positive values of pain; for unless viewed from the perspective of time and the larger experience of living, pain is destructive. It has a way of teaching many lessons when we are willing to accept them. It was ten years after a severe illness before I came to appreciate what I had learned there.

A woman I know had been in the hospital for three years; during that time she had suffered great pain for prolonged periods of time. One day she said, "Mr. Dicks, I would not have missed this experience for the world." I said, "What do you mean?" She said, "Through this experience of being ill and suffering I have found a faith. When I became ill I did not believe in prayer or know how to pray. Now I do." Her quiet endurance in the midst of her suffering verified her statement; unfortunately others, many others go through such experiences with different results. Some have faith at the outset but lose it during their suffering. In fact, I believe that most people who have an active faith and drop out of the church do so because no one steadied them during a period of personal crisis.

B. FEAR

Fear is the second type of personal crisis we recognize in people. Dr. Joseph Fort Newton has said that more people have written him over the years about fear, on the basis of his syndicated articles, than any other problem. The difference between fear, apprehension and worry is one of degree, although the bodily changes are different in that they are more pronounced in fear than in apprehension, but their cause is the same.

The fear of being afraid is the problem of the soldier. When the American troops first landed in Africa they were green troops, despite the fact that they had been trained for such action for months. I was with some of those troops before they sailed; they were cocky and confident. On maneuvers they had performed ably, taking their objectives, and solving their field problems easily, yet as the ships were shelled when they approached the time for the amphibious attack some of the men fell upon the deck crying, "Mother, mother!" It was not many weeks, however, until they were driving the Germans into the sea; they had overcome their fear and were once again performing effectively.

One type of fear is the easily recognized condition which is acute fear. This is basic and primitive. We hold this emotion in common with other creatures. It is the body's preparation for combat or for flight. As civilized creatures, we have overcome some of the need for such strong emotions but we still have the same capacity for being frightened our forefathers had many centuries and ages ago. The result is that these feelings often get out of control and do us harm through worry.

There is the second type of fear, not so easily recognized but which is devastating in its effect; this is apprehension, which is the kind of fear that keeps us awake nights. It is closely tied up with guilt feelings, which I will discuss presently. Further, I believe there is a close tie-up between worry and one's attitude toward death, which also would lead us to feel that worry ties up with guilt feelings. When we worry about a loved one's possible death we are afraid of loneliness and the loss of affection and companionship. Apprehension gnaws away at one's poise and faith until one breaks completely, thus seeking relief from suffering in the insensibility of a psychosis, or so-called nervous breakdown.

At one Army air training base where there had been several crashes I was told that the men had become afraid of the planes. At another Naval air-training base it is a common thing for the cadets to get the jitters shortly before they graduate, after they have demonstrated their ability to fly. The fear of "washing out" would not account for this condition; only a deeper apprehension that ties up more closely with the realization that combat assignments are near, would account for such anxiety. The cause of the apprehension is lost to consciousness and sometimes must await further suffering to bring it to the surface.

The opposite of fear is faith, confidence that the world at its heart can be trusted. Some persons seem never to have been afraid, others seem to be afraid of everything, while most of us are in between, afraid sometimes and of some things, not afraid at other times. Certainly it is the part of wisdom to be afraid at times. The good soldier is one who is capable of fear, otherwise he takes unnecessary risks. The story has been told of the veteran soldier walking beside the rookie as they went into combat. The rookie looked at the color of the veteran's face and said, "You're afraid?" "Yes," replied the veteran, "if you were only half as scared as I am you would run away."

I have seen some persons go into the operating room frightened so badly they could not speak, others go calmly, relaxed and at ease. This latter is a condition that is hard come by and one that grows out of the practice of faith and learning to trust. As one woman put it, "It's all right whether I get well or whether I don't, it's all right!" That was no easy resignation, but a statement of faith which she had gained through long hours of prayer.

Contrast that statement with the situation of another woman I knew who could tell you the day, hour and place where she was "saved," yet she was afraid to go home. One of these women was simply more advanced in her faith and acceptance of God than the other.

C. GUILT FEELINGS

Guilt feelings are closely tied up with fear; still if it were possible to remove all fear we would still have a feeling that could be identified as a *sense of failure*. Guilt feelings underlie much of living; they are potentially present in all our decisions and behavior. We seldom are definitely conscious of a "sense of the ought," still it is the background against which we live. Without this background we would not have developed the kind of human society we have and hope to have. Just as the emotions of pain and fear make the human creature one with other creatures, so the emotion of guilt—the capacity to feel sorrow for an act—sets man apart from other creatures.

There may be many more but we can identify at least two

kinds, or levels, of guilt feelings: the conscious level is one, while the unconscious sense of failure is the other. The first is apt to turn upon a single act, sometimes of a superficial nature; the second may be a single act but it is the result of cumulative thought and brooding. It is the athletic player fouling an opponent on the spur of the moment but doing it in such a way as to reveal that the act had been carefully planned, so that at the moment there was little conscious thought in the act.

A flying instructor and a cadet walked into the chaplain's office at an air base. Their faces were flushed, they were tense and nervous, obviously under considerable emotional stress. The instructor said, "Chaplain, did you hear about the crash?" "No," the chaplain replied, "has there been a crash?" "Yes, another plane pulled in front of ours as we were taking off. It crashed and the pilot was killed. It seemed as if we were at least partially responsible. We thought we would like you to have a prayer with us and read the twenty-third Psalm." This is an illustration of conscious guilt feelings as well as a request for specific treatment.

Contrast this with another story similar in its setting. Two men were flying a light bomber when the plane broke in two; the pilot ordered the co-pilot to bail out; the latter ran to the back of the plane and parachuted to safety. Just before he jumped he looked back and saw the pilot struggling to unhook a strap of his parachute harness which was caught on some gadget. The plane crashed and the pilot was killed. The co-pilot who had parachuted to safety found his way to the chaplain's office a few days after the accident, although he did not know why he came to the chaplain. He wanted to talk about the experience but did not understand why. Actually he was assuming responsibility for the death of his pilot; without realizing it, he felt he should have gone back and helped his friend.

If it were pointed out that he had no time to do so and, if he had, both would have lost their lives, he would have answered that that did not matter, he should not have jumped until the other man was free.

A soldier who was greatly depressed sought out a U. S. O. director with the words, "I am responsible for my buddie's death." When he was encouraged to talk he told the story of his friend who had come into town the week before with another soldier. They got some liquor, stole a truck, turned it over and both were killed. When asked why he felt responsible for his friend's death the soldier replied, "Because I could have kept him from getting into trouble. He never got drunk when I was with him." When asked why he had not come into town that night he replied he had been on duty and could not get off. It was pointed out that since he was on duty and since it was not his decision that had kept him from being with his friend when the latter was killed, it was not his fault. The soldier still persisted, "Nevertheless, it was my fault he was killed."

We should not expect these stories to make sense, or for a person to be reasonable when he is suffering from a sense of guilt. Guilt feelings are no more reasonable than are other emotions.

Guilt feelings and religion are tied up together, for it is the function of the church to describe goals of living, to hold up the ideal. The church constantly emphasizes the "ought," the way life may be lived but seldom is; organized religion works to maintain tensions within us lest we become possessed with comfort and indifference to the needs of others.

As individuals we may go through experiences of crisis and suffering quite apart from the nation's sufferings, so that the church's practice should not be determined by the nation's condition, although its predominant message may well be. As individuals we experience this sense of failure on many occasions and we naturally look to the church for help.

If suffering of guilt feelings is prolonged without relief then people turn away from the church. The free churches, particularly, have not been realistic or helpful in their dealing with guilt feelings. They have thought it was their task to bring people to a "conviction of sin," believing that when people have suffered sufficiently they will turn to the church and God. They even recognize that one may backslide and still return for forgiveness.

The liturgical churches are more realistic in their dealing with guilt feelings through the practice of confession. If confession is consistently practised the sense of guilt is not apt to become so deep-rooted and is therefore more easily relieved; also the individual communicant knows he can receive help through the church and is therefore more healthy-minded. The great strength of the confessional, however, is that the individual knows where to find someone who will listen to his trouble and listen understandingly.

I do not mean to suggest that our only concern with guilt should be to relieve it, although that seems to be the attitude of some who work in allied professions. Some psychiatrists and social workers claim a sense of guilt only makes a person sick; such an attitude represents a superficial knowledge of living. How long would government hold together without a sense of responsibility? Not long. In fact democracy today faces a serious threat because more people capable of this sense of responsibility, with its corresponding capacity for feeling a sense of guilt, do not go into government work while the more basic indifference rests back upon the voters themselves and their failure to exercise the franchise. The same thing can be said about other phases of our life and living.

Guilt feelings may lead to action; but unless that action is wisely chosen then tragedy is the result. It is the function of the clergyman to direct the actions which are motivated by guilt feelings. Many clergy fail in this task because they do not know what they are dealing with; others fail because of their own biases, prejudices and suppressed guilt feelings.

Gradually the physician's consultation has been substituted for the ancient rite of confession and from that have come other substitutions until now the medical profession has largely taken over the care of the total person. Today the clergy is facing expulsion from the very task that brought it into existence: the care of souls. It gains little to sit back and point out the failures of the doctor with his limited conception of life, in his spiritual care of individuals. He is at work at the task; the same cannot always be said of the clergy.

D. LONELINESS

Loneliness underlies more human behavior than any other emotion unless it is hunger. It is not as primitive as fear and therefore not as basic but in our generation it is far more general. Loneliness permeates the whole of life; it stimulates the child's love for its parents, it is the prime emotion behind courtship, it leads to the establishing of homes and communities, for it is the background of love, it is the problem of the aged and it is the problem of bereavement. Loneliness causes us to seek new experience, to turn to adventure, to bow in worship. When in the clasp of loneliness we may become depressed or we may become aggressive.

In the military situation we see loneliness in its acute form; specifically it is homesickness. It leads to boredom and poor morale. Ninety per cent of life in the Army is waiting for something to happen. A Navy chaplain who served with the

Marines in Samoa told me men would just walk the streets on their off duty time. Many times he would take a man by the arm and say to him, "Go in there and look at that movie!" "Go out there and get into that ball game!" A sergeant in charge of recreation for his regiment told me they had had no trouble because they had a well planned recreation program. Once he had taken twelve men who had gone A. W. O. L. and planned a show with them; those that could perform did the acting— those who had no ability became stage hands. It was their show and it was a good one; for the first time some of them seemed content in the Army.

Loneliness underlies some rather peculiar behavior. I was told of a college girl whose clothes were untidy, whose hair was never fixed, and who always needed a bath. The psychologist would explain such a person's actions or her failure to care for her person on the basis of attitudes she held toward her family, where there was little affection. She built up an attitude of "Nobody loves me; I'm an ugly duckling." It was not surprising that she was failing in school, that she had no dates, that she had no friends. Her basic problem was *loneliness*.

There are at least two kinds of loneliness that we can identify. There is a superficial, nagging, gnawing kind such as homesickness, such as the lover desiring to be with the loved one. While this is a disturbing feeling and may lead one to dire actions and desperate behavior in extreme instances, by and large it is handled fairly well by most persons. It is a condition which we recognize is temporary and nothing that a little pluck and endurance will not handle. If prolonged over a period of time without relief it may lead to serious mental depressions in some; in others it is apt to seek relief through aggressive acts such as drinking and fighting. In some girls it leads to depression, to worry, to anxiety, to sickness; in others it leads to aggressive acts toward men, to drinking, to sexual laxness.

There is a second type of loneliness which is more basic in nature and more difficult to identify. It is the kind the girl, described above, illustrates which rests back upon earlier experiences in the home; which is usually on a subconscious level so that the person himself does not know what causes him to act as he does. Psychologists believe it is this feeling that causes body odor, bad breath and other forms of repulsive conditions to develop within and about a person. In one girl with whom I counseled about her pending divorce, which she ultimately secured, lack of affection between her mother and father had caused her to make an early, unfortunate marriage. She married to get away from her home where there was always quarreling and because her parents gave her little affection, for they did not have it to give. She married the first man who asked her, and from her description of him, despite her efforts to the contrary, he seemed to be rather a desirable fellow. Once married and away from her mother and father, she found it impossible to feel real affection for her husband because she would not let herself love or be loved. She did not know how. She had two babies but felt little affection for them. At heart she is a lonely person and it is doubtful if she will ever be anything else. Religion attracted her early in life and while she gained much from it, it tended to increase her loneliness rather than relieve it because religion is based upon faith, trust, love. These she did not know. While she was an attractive girl she went to great pains to make herself unattractive through the way she did her hair and the way she wore her clothes. Curiously enough, she was not bitter and her personality was rather pleasant.

It is this deep loneliness that is baffling and for which we have little effective treatment. This is the kind of frustration and restlessness that has turned out explorers and adventurers, searchers, wanderers and geniuses. The great saints and the great sinners both have been sired by this kind of loneliness.

CHAPTER IX

RAPPORT

THE emotional relationship between two or more persons, when it is satisfying, is called *rapport*. This is a word which originates in the French psychiatry literature. It denotes a feeling of goodwill, friendliness, confidence, trust, affection; in its deeper sense, it means love. The word, by definition, is positive; it does not carry a negative equivalent. When there is a feeling of resentment, dislike, ill will or hatred we say, "There is no rapport present." You will readily recognize that this is an understatement in many situations.

I was asked to see a very sick girl by her physician. When I walked into her room she looked at me and said, "Who are you?" I said, "I'm the minister of the hospital." She said, "I don't like ministers." To describe the feeling set up immediately between us as lack of friendliness would be an understatement. So long as the feeling is not mutual the ill will or dislike soon gives way to rapport, which happened in the above instance. As soon as I demonstrated to her that I had not come to have a "long" prayer with her, her attitude toward me changed. There came the time when her nurse would send for me instead of her physician, and for the specific purpose of having a prayer with her. It was not that she disliked ministers, it was only that she did not like her own minister who did two things that upset her; he always reviewed his last Sunday's sermon when he called, which characterized him as a conceited person, and she said he always prayed "an hour." Beyond that she had had trouble with him because of the choir; if it had not been for that trouble the other mistakes might have been forgiven him.

Rapport is all-important in pastoral work. In fact it is the *most* important factor in bringing about healing and in gaining a feeling of emotional security. Much has been written about friendship. Rapport is the experience of friendship. A patient I knew over a long and trying period of time said, " want you to come to me as a friend, not as a minister." The two cannot be separated, however. I would not have had the occasion to see him at all except as I was a minister. Dr. Samuel Kincheloe of the Chicago Theological Seminary has called the pastor's task, "professionalized friendliness." That is well put providing there is not too much professionalism about it. There should be enough to guard against a sticky and sickly sentimentality. One boy said, "I want you to come to see me because you care about *me*, not because you love Christ."

Some ministers who are afraid of affection, especially when it comes from a woman, retreat behind a love of Christ. Their work is ineffective, not because they love Christ so much but because they do not love Him enough, for one who really loves Christ deeply does not need to fear love from an emotional woman. Loving Christ does not mean that our affection is worn on our coat sleeve. The love of Christ is what carries us to the side of those who are suffering; without it we have not the courage to go.

The minister, physician, nurse, social worker, teacher, cannot help a person unless rapport is present. This is especially true of the minister's work because so much of it lies in the emotional area. There are certain things which a doctor may do for his patient, minor things, like giving a physic, that are not dependent upon affection between the patient and physician. This is not true when it comes to a rapid and satisfactory recovery from an operation; some persons die because the surgeon and his assistants neglect their patients' attitudes. A nurse can make a bed, and do it well without her patient liking her but her patient's recovery will be retarded by just so much as she is disliked. A social worker may give a client money for relief but if the client is made to feel unworthy, forces of resentment that are far reaching are set in action. A teacher whose pupils do not like her is a liability and a drag upon education. Rapport, this feeling of friendliness, runs through the whole of life and living.

A basic teaching of the Hebrew and Christian religions is that the universe at its heart is friendly. There are few original teachings in the message of Jesus; perhaps His outstanding contribution was His understanding of the Mind and Nature of God. Friendliness, affection, love are the characteristics of God as Jesus described Him. In our own suffering we feel that the world has gone back on us, is indifferent to our suffering or is against us; we have this feeling regardless of how much God through nature is working in our behalf. This attitude toward the Universe, or God, is affected by our feelings for those around us. There is a natural desire within us to feel a kinship with nature and with people; we are naturally friendly. When, through suffering, we turn bitter and resentful it is because we do not have the emotional support which affection gives us. Rapport renews faith, thus overcoming fear; rapport, as felt between parishioner and minister, expresses confidence through an attitude of "neither do I condemn thee," when the parishioner is suffering from guilt feelings. The parishioner believes that the minister sees with the eyes of God, thus he may be relieved more readily by the minister's affection than by anyone's else. Rapport, by its very nature, breaks the clasp of loneliness. The rapport, rather than what the pastor says, makes pastoral work helpful in three of the crisis areas of life as described in chapter VIII.

Rapport is important in pastoral work and preaching because we do not think with our minds, we think with our feelings; we are not moved by ideas, we are moved by our emotions; we do not reach decisions with our heads, we reach them with our hearts. Therefore, to influence a person you must have his affection. If a congregation likes its minister he is the greatest preacher in the world; if it dislikes him there is nothing he can do that is commendable, no sermon he can preach worth listening to. Some of our reformers might remember that; it is not a question of whether their causes are desirable or not. Rather it is that they are more interested in the cause than in the people it affects.

Rapport develops in relation and in proportion to the needs for rapport on the part of two people. Its degree is determined by the need for affection and support of those experiencing the rapport, for affection *is* support. This need is determined by the stress or suffering, immediate and past, of the persons coming into the rapport-experience. The surgeon establishes rapport easily and quickly because of the patient's complete dependence upon him. Trust in one's surgeon is a blind, unquestioning trust—it must be or one would never permit himself to be operated upon. This rapport may be strong on the patient's part, if the surgeon is interested primarily in the technical job of removing disease through surgery, and does not include the patient as a person. The rapport may lessen when the patient recovers health and may remain quiescent until further need arises.

Religion develops out of man's deep need for fellowship with God, for a satisfactory and satisfying relationship to the world in which he lives. The pastor's task is to aid in working out that relationship. The ancient church fathers thought this role was of vital importance; Protestantism has never been

illing to admit that it was. Clinical psychology, with its prag-
matic approach to life, observes every day that man does need
nd is constantly seeking help in this task of establishing his
roper relationship with God and with his environment. He
eeds help because life is complicated and because suffering
isrupts the basic tendency to believe and trust the Universe.
ince affection is a stabilizing force and since the pastor is
alled to his task and ordained to his role of serving God the
ffection which is felt for him may be a unique and soul-
strengthening force; to be helpful this affection must be re-
urned by the pastor. I will discuss the pastor's part in rapport
more fully in the following chapter.

A. SIGNS OF RAPPORT

The tone of voice, the eyes, the face, the head, the content of
peech, the hands and the body reveal rapport. In America
ustom dictates that two persons who are introduced shake
ands; custom does not dictate whether they shall smile or not,
or what they shall say beyond the introduction. The person
who treats you pleasantly, who responds to your interest, who
alls your name, who makes an effort to please you, expresses
is goodwill toward you which indicates that the condition
pon which rapport may be built is present. The harsh voice,
he abrupt and rude expression, the lack of pleasantness, the
ailure to shake hands, the indifference to your presence ex-
resses defensiveness and lack of rapport. A person who is
ggressively direct in his speech and manner is on the defensive
nd may be quite unstable emotionally, just as the "witty"
erson may be, and any rapport that is established is apt to be
uperficial and undependable because of the unstable nature
f the aggressive person.

B. Establishing Rapport

In pastoral work and personal counseling rapport is established and strengthened by what the clergyman is able to avoid doing as well as by what he does after the beginning is made. This is one of the most delicate phases of pastoral work, for the minister works from a bias; he is opposed to certain behavior, attitudes, opinions. How to overcome the prejudice engendered by his position in relation to those whose behavior is different and who hold opinions which are at variance with the clergyman's calls for the greatest of skill. Some clergy say frankly they do not care to associate with persons who hold different opinions; we need to remember that our Lord came not to associate with saints.

One day I was lecturing before a group of Negro ministers upon the importance of rapport when one of the group got very uncomfortable. Finally he broke in, "How are you going to keep their affection when you got to hurt them?" he asked. "When they do wrong you got to hurt them. That's the way God does." His question is a searching one, perhaps one of the most searching.

When a child does wrong we know we do him no favor, in fact we do him an injustice, in overlooking his act. At the same time if we punish him in anger we do both him and ourselves an injustice. For three years I called upon a thirty-one-year-old man who was very resentful. His bitterness was so intense that his recovery was retarded by it. He blamed another man for the injury which had confined him to his bed and later to a wheel chair and which necessitated one operation after another. He even interviewed an attorney and made plans to sue but never could quite bring himself to the point of starting proceedings. Day after day and week after week I called upon him; time after time he poured forth his bitterness and often he spoke of starting legal action. While I recognized the cause of his injury, I could never believe the accident had been caused either by neglect or malicious intent on the part of the person my friend blamed for his condition. After nearly three years the patient began to improve. One day he said, "You never disagreed with me, I could never have stood that. Neither did you ever agree with me."

We do not have to defend our position by expressed opinion; neither dare we compromise it. Rapport is strengthened by our genuine interest in a person; that in itself blossoms into affection. Jesus seems, above all others, to have had the ability to attract people to him through his affection for them. His teachings are striking in their simplicity, human in their appeal, but even his teachings vibrate his affection for those around him. He simply loved people into the kingdom.

The building of rapport and the strengthening of rapport is slow and tedious and it is only possible when we are afire with love. As God's assistants we serve as the conductor of His love which flows through us like electricity flowing through high-tension wires. Rapport is balanced between the parishioner and his need for help and the pastor and his need to help. When these two needs are nearly equal rapport is established; if the need for help outweighs the need to help, pastoral work fails.

CHAPTER X

THE CLERGYMAN

THE third condition that makes for effective pastoral work is the spiritual maturity of the pastor. As one sick woman expressed it, "I was all right until my pastor called, but he was so ill at ease and jittery that the first thing I knew he had me that way. He was worse off than I was. I thought I ought to get up and give him my bed." If we are worse off than those we try to help it is certain we will not be able to be of any benefit to them; for we must be living examples of the faith we represent.

Just as stress judges the person going through the suffering, so it tests the faith of the pastor who comes into the crisis as a pastor. Certainly God did not deliberately bring the war about even though He created a world in which war is inevitable under certain conditions, just as the cross was inevitable for Jesus because of existing conditions at Jerusalem. Once war was declared, however, to turn one's back upon it, to refuse to admit that it was going on was to play an unrealistic part. That would not be God's way of acting. Those clergy who went into the armed services as chaplains demonstrated their faith and their concern for God's people. One of the conditions of the chaplain's effectiveness is his own spiritual poise and maturity of soul in the suffering which he faces in the war.

When I first met Dr. Richard C. Cabot, to talk about going to the Massachusetts General Hospital as chaplain, he said, "Why are you interested in sick people?" I said, "Because I have been sick myself." His reply was blunt and to the point, and he could be very much to the point upon occasion, "I'm glad you have." At another time I remember his saying, "If I had my way I would see to it that every doctor, nurse, social worker, and clergyman became seriously ill themselves. They'd know something about their jobs then." It was not important that he had never had a day's illness in his life; his point still stood and in this he was right. Out of suffering comes maturity of soul and the need to help others who suffer. It is doubtful if any person reaches a depth of living, an appreciation for life, a spiritual quietness and poise, without suffering—the type of suffering whether it be pain, fear, guilt feelings, loneliness, does not matter. If Richard Cabot had said "suffering" instead of "illness" he would have included himself, for he had known other suffering than physical pain.

Spiritual maturity comes from having prayed. There are as many ways of praying as there are many types of suffering. Many times we pray significantly for the first time when we suffer. Acute suffering, such as a parent knows when a child is seriously ill, may cause us to pray heatedly; but we may not really pray until the child dies. Then our faith is truly expanded although there may be no uttered word. Formally we prayed for God to give the child health that we might help him; now we pray that we may trust God to keep him, love him as a parent loves him. Formerly our faith in God was passive, we desired that He support us; now it becomes active, for we pray for faith to trust God to care for the child as we would.

To pray to God for the relief of suffering is one thing; to understand and accept the reason why pain is not relieved is quite another. The heated moment must be seen against the background of eternity. That is perspective. Spiritual maturity, quietness of soul is gained through the acquiring of a perspective. "A thousand years in Thy sight, O Lord."

In the two preceding chapters we have discussed the parishioner's spiritual needs, on the one hand, and the rapport between the parishioner and the pastor as a healing experience, on the other. We have not asked the question, how does the pastor come by spiritual poise that enables him to uphold his part of the rapport. Our pastors of the past have spoken of being "called"; I would hold to that conception. We are called through our suffering, through our frustration, through our need for love of man and love of God. The person who loves God but does not love his fellow creatures should not be a pastor; neither should he be a preacher. Let him become cloistered where he may adore God as he will best know how, but for him to be ordained to the pastoral ministry would be a sad mistake. One's frustration must not be so complete that he is unconscious of the suffering of others.

The first step in gaining spiritual maturity is the mastery of the physical organism. The physical organism is mastered through the mind; playing one against the other will master both. Physical relaxation in time of stress is gained through practicing physical relaxation which calls for mental discipline. The art of physical relaxation should be learned when free from stress, although many people do not bother to learn relaxation until some need arises for it. The high wire and trapeze artist is a symphony of the mastery of mind over muscle. The singing artist must be able to master the physical instrument through physical relaxation. That alone does not make a great singer; no technique will make a master craftsman of any art—but a singer cannot be a great singer without having mastered the technique. Physical relaxation is a significant part of the art of prayer, for profound prayer grows out of quietness.[1]

Through your ability to relax you demonstrate your faith in the world in which you live. If you are ill at ease; if you act

[1] See *You Must Relax*, Jacobson. New edition, Whittlesey House, New York, 1943.

and feel insecure and afraid you belie the very faith in you. Read the 35th Psalm, verse 5, "Trust now thyself to God." The trouble is we do not know how to trust. Relaxing is a letting go, a giving over of tension, of decision, of apprehension. It is trusting the chair upon which you sit, the bed upon which you lie, the floor upon which you stand; not often will they give way under you. Faith is trusting your heart to beat, your blood to circulate through your body, your digestive tract to do its work and eliminate its waste. Constipation is a sign of lack of faith, of spiritual immaturity; just as "bad breath" is a sign of worry. If as a pastor you would demonstrate your faith, do not worry about what you will say; your actions may belie your words. Prepare first your soul through learning to trust God in simple things. The simple things of living are the important things, after all, for they are the only ones over which we have control.

The pastor's spiritual poise is affected vitally by the kind of marriage he makes. Marriage may be a spiritually stabilizing experience or it may be spiritually frustrating. Ministers make as many, and some believe more, bad marriages, than anyone else. This is because they are idealistic and naïve.

Spiritual poise is developed through study and meditation. This study will cover many fields. It will cover the deep nature of God and the ways of God, as revealed through nature around us, through direct observation. Beyond that it will include the study of God, as revealed through the observations of others, particularly the men of science who search for truth. Especially it will include study of the lives of those devoted to religious meditation and study. First, last and always it will include a study of the life and teachings of the Central Figure of Christianity.

Without the fire which is released in us through the passion and affection of our Lord as the Central Figure in our efforts to help other people we will never develop a quietness of soul which will enable us really to help others. Much pastoral work fails because we have not come to be possessed by His devotion to this task.

It must possess us but at the same time it must be disciplined; through this devotion we know the peace which passeth understanding. Pastoral work is helpful in so far as the minister has drunk of the water of eternal life, which we know through our devotion to Jesus Christ. His own words give the secret to effective pastoral work, "Whosoever shall lose his life for my sake, and the gospel's, shall save it." When we lose ourselves in Him and His cause we have reached a spiritual maturity that enables us to enter into the emotional relationship of rapport with a quietness of soul that reflects the Spirit of Him who said, "Come unto me, all ye that labor and are heavy laden and I will give you rest."

PART FOUR

THE ART OF PASTORAL WORK

CHAPTER XI

LISTENING

FOR some years there has been a dispute over the relative importance of *methods* in pastoral work and *insight* which underlies pastoral work. Dr. Anton Boisen, beloved father of the clinical training movement for theological students, in his teaching and writing has always emphasized the importance of understanding human personality as the key to effective pastoral work and counseling. I, however, maintain that we should emphasize a sound method first, believing that our insight will develop as we work. Most of the leaders in the clinical training movement have followed Dr. Boisen, although some have included both viewpoints.[1]

Dr. Boisen's field of interest has been the mental hospital and psycho-pathology; he has worked with psychiatrists and psychoanalysts and has followed their writings closely. My interest and field of study has been the general hospital and the near-normal person. I have worked intimately with the general practising physician and surgeon and while I have studied psychiatry and drawn generally from its analysis of human personality I have not followed the psycho-therapist closely, as I believe the clergyman must ultimately make his own analysis of his work.

The first principle which the general physician and surgeon follow is: *do no harm.* Early in my work as chaplain in a general hospital this also became my first principle. In my teaching of theological students I have stressed this point; naturally it

[1] *Religion and Health,* Hiltner. The Macmillan Company, New York, 1943.

led readily to a description of and emphasis upon methods. I have described what to do, what not to do, depicting methods of carrying on one's work without doing harm, assured in the knowledge that if that were accomplished we would help most of our people.

My contention is that if a minister learns a few basic methods of pastoral work and gains an understanding of the underlying conditions that make for effective pastoral work he will be able to help people. He has a lifetime to study human personality and deepen his understanding but he must start his work with people immediately, when he accepts leadership in a church.

Naturally, to use any method some understanding of human personality is necessary, and the greater the understanding the more effectively will be the minister's use of his method. One shudders at the thought of the limited experience and lack of knowledge that our clergy have as they go out to work with people. If our doctors were not better trained than our clergy we would not let them treat our dogs, to say nothing of our children; yet a suffering soul is more important than a suffering body, a broken heart infinitely more significant than a broken leg.

The doctor studies anatomy before he studies the technique of surgery; he studies the bones and nerves and muscles of a leg before he studies how to set a bone that has been fractured. Ideally psycho-pathology should be studied first. The difference between the physician and the clergyman is that the doctor has been keeping records, analyzing his work and studying his failures for a hundred and fifty years. Only now is the clergyman coming to the place where he admits that he has ever failed, or dares to subject his work to the discipline of records. Most books, even of recent date, in the general pastoral work field, do not admit failure. This shows the naïveté of our observers and writers.

In our present development we must do as the doctor has done through the generations; we must work as best we can with our present understanding of our task, giving attention to doing as little harm as possible, knowing that God through nature is working on our side. At the same time we must work to increase our knowledge and understanding of human personality and behavior.

A famous pastor has given us the story of a girl who came to him saying, "Doctor, I want to talk to you about my lack of belief in God." The pastor said, "Tell me first about that love affair." His insight was excellent; his method was poor. He moved too fast. The girl's reaction was certain to have been, "My God, is it that obvious!" Good pastoral work does not shock the parishioner; the risk of doing harm is too great. Hence the importance of sound methods which temper insight.

In my early days as chaplain at the Massachusetts General Hospital in Boston I went about seeing patients suffering from various diseases. Because I did not know what to say, and had little chance to say it even if I had known, I kept quiet and let the patients talk, which they did readily enough. They talked about themselves and their suffering; they talked about their families and homes, and sometimes their lack of family and home; they talked about their jobs and their bosses, jobs they had done and other jobs they hoped to secure; they talked about places they had been, people they had met, books they had read and sometimes books they had written or hoped to write; they talked about sports, baseball, hockey, prize fights, and football; they talked about their churches and their ministers; and again they talked about themselves, their loneliness, their fears, their frustrations, their beliefs and lack of beliefs; they talked of death and of dying, their fear of dying and their eagerness to die. These patients were strangers but a brief time before; now they talked willingly, readily, frankly and eagerly. When I rose to go they thanked me for having helped them. They did seem to have been helped. When I asked myself what I had done the answer was obvious: I had listened.

Psychiatrists, psycho-analysts and social workers have talked of listening. The ancient church made it a Sacrament. Little has been said of it among the free churches since the Reformation. Our clergy have spoken of themselves as "called to preach," by which they have meant proclaiming the gospel, pointing the way. Preaching is preacher-centered while listening is parishioner-centered. Listening means the sufferer selects the topic of conversation, raises questions, seeks for the answers. Listening means working with a parishioner where *he* is in his soul's journey, not where the pastor is. Listening means patience and courage and trust in the universe of which we are a part. Ministers are usually poor listeners because they have thought of their calling as being in another direction, the opposite of listening, the opposite of pastoral work, yet the essence of good pastoral work is good listening It is easier to preach than it is to be a pastor, for talking is easier than listening. When I talk, I talk about myself and my interests, when I listen I hear you talk about yours.

Occasionally I hear a pastor describe his work with a parishioner by saying, "All I did was listen!" *All* I did was listen. I want to say, "Brother, you will never do anything more important, anything more helpful, or anything more difficult, *if, if* only you did listen."

Underlying listening are the three conditions which were described in Section III: suffering on the part of the parishioner; rapport, which is probably the most important single factor in the healing, creative ministry of listening; and the stability and soul-poise of the listener. Recognizing these three underlying conditions of listening, let us move on to describe it more specifically as a method. I have made various efforts at describing listening as a method in pastoral work. Each time I add more to the description.

A. Passive Listening

Passive listening is characterized by the pastor being passive while the parishioner talks, unfolding his story, taking his time, making his transitions, getting off the subject, weeping, cursing, continuing. It does not mean that the listener goes to sleep, or sits like a hulk, it does not mean, as Seward Hiltner has said, "demonstrating our strength by outstaring the parishioner" by looking him steadily in the eye. It means being alert; it means nodding your head encouragingly; it means looking past the parishioner and out the window or over his head at the wall; it means looking at the parishioner and looking away; it means waiting and hoping; it means relaxing within your physical body so as not to block the story through your own resistance and prejudice; it means trusting God and believing that good can come out of evil and hope out of suffering. Passive listening is aided by the use of the eyes, the face, the alertness of the body even as it is relaxed, and above all by little grunts of *ah* and *um*, and *um huh*.

Passive listening is the kind of listening used in the formal confessional. The difference in our use of it and the priest's in the confessional is that confession, as practiced in the liturgical churches, is strictly regulated by canon law and is formalized around the commandments. Thus the priest may not get at the underlying causes of behavior but deals only with the overt act. If, as modern psychology teaches, all behavior is purposeful, then the overt act may be quite insignificant. For example, lying is defensive behavior from the psychologist's point of view. The fact that you have lied is one thing, but the reason for the lie is quite another. From the standpoint of theology a lie is a sin; from the standpoint of psychology it may be the key to an underlying problem which may become serious unless understood and dealt with. Many a mother, upon discovering that her son has lied to her, fears he is headed for the state penitentiary. He may be headed for the penitentiary, or the psychopathic hospital unless the causes of his lying, one link in a chain of behavior, can be examined. Passive listening is the method which we use in relieving surface stress in order to get at the underlying causes of behavior; once this is discovered a more aggressive type of listening may be required.

B. ACTIVE LISTENING

Active, or directed, listening is characterized by the use of questions by the pastor. What the scalpel is to the surgeon the question is to the pastoral counselor, and it is quite as dangerous. The good surgical operator is one who knows what to cut and what not to cut, and who has a knowledge of time; the good pastor is one who knows what to ask and what not to ask, plus a feel for timeliness. To ask one's questions too rapidly is like the surgeon who cuts into an abdomen too fast.

The art of pastoral work is the ability to know which questions to ask, and when. Through the use of questions we express our interest in a person, we explore his spiritual condition, we relieve suffering, we reveal and aid in the gaining of insight, we release new resources, we stimulate new efforts. The art of asking questions is the art of pastoral work.

I discovered the use of questions, called psycho-therapy, in a state mental hospital while I was still an undergraduate.

Shortly after my return to the seminary, a new student, who had returned to finish his preparation for the ministry after spending eight years in business, came to my room. He said, "I heard the boys say you have been studying psychology and counseling. I need some help." We went to work in the way I remembered the psychiatrists asked questions. I asked him why he had left the seminary eight years before, why he had returned, why he went into business, how successful he was in business, why he got married, whether he loved his wife, if they were happily married, why they had a child and whether his wife was in love with someone else, all in less than half an hour. At the end of that time he jumped up and practically ran out of my room. I did not see him again for a conference for over a week despite his acute need for counseling. That is the way we do harm when, through the use of aggressive questions, we have no consciousness of time. Those were good questions but they should have been spread over a period of several conferences, which would have given rapport and time an opportunity to heal his wounds. When the rapport is sufficiently strong there is no problem of being too aggressive, because, as said in chapter IX, rapport develops in relation to the need for help and the capacity of the pastor to help.

Through the use of questions we explore a person's spiritual condition; at the same time insight is developed in the parishioner. The baffling fact remains, however, that some persons are helped through talking about themselves even though little insight is gained.

C. INTERPRETATION

A third phase of the listening method may be called interpretation. Some writers speak of interpretation as a separate method. This seems to me to be a mistake for the simple reason that without listening there would be nothing to interpret.

Interpretation in pastoral work is a short-cut method and is used primarily because the pastor is pushed for time and because his *active-listening* method has broken down. Sometimes it is necessary to use interpretation because our people have no conception of how they may be helped through pastoral work. They come seeking advice, and advice they expect to receive, because they are accustomed to being told what to do, or because they want the responsibility of a decision to be carried by someone else. In some rare instances advice is desirable for the reason that the responsibility of a decision is too great for the person seeking help.

Interpretation is characterized by the pastor explaining underlying causes of behavior which the parishioner may not be conscious of or understand. It has certain risks that *active listening* does not have because the pastor stakes all upon being right in his interpretation and he works upon the assumption that the parishioner will accept it. In this assumption he may be wrong regardless of the truth of his interpretation. A fact may be a fact in reality and to the pastor's knowledge, but unless it is accepted as a fact by the parishioner the pastor must recognize the limitation of its reality and work with the parishioner in his conception of it.

A mother wrote to a Navy chaplain of her son's failure to answer her letters or to acknowledge the gifts she had sent him. When the chaplain talked with the sailor, who had an excellent service record, he admitted his failure to write his mother, saying he had been quite busy, but promised to do so soon. When later the mother came to the camp, traveling from a distant city, the sailor in talking to her over the telephone at first reported he could not see her at all because of training restrictions. The mother appealed to the chaplain who called in the son; the son then said he would see his mother the following day for Sunday dinner at her hotel. He could have secured leave at nine o'clock, instead he arranged to meet his mother at one. At three o'clock he had not arrived. The mother went to the bus station to watch for him, finally she saw him getting on a bus to return to camp. She spoke to him and he reluctantly got off the bus and talked to her. When she asked him where he had been he said he had gone to the hotel but could not find her; when she asked if he had had his lunch he said that he had. She asked him to go with her while she ate. A few minutes later he explained that he must return to the camp and left. The next day the mother, now nearly frantic, called upon the chaplain and explained what had happened the day before. The chaplain asked numerous questions of her, then he called the son in for a talk. The sailor was at a loss to explain his behavior, which he admitted was strange. The chaplain had formulated his own theory of the mother-son relationship, having discovered the lad was an only son and that his mother had doted on and spoiled him all his life.

Now the chaplain faced a choice in the method he would use in his final conference with the mother. He could, through the use of questions, attempt to lead her to discover how in her past over-indulgent relationship with her son she had tied him to herself emotionally, so that when he came into the Navy, where the ability to stand upon one's own feet is rated highly, he found his mother had failed to prepare him for his present hard assignment. Without realizing just what he was doing the son had been blindly trying to break his emotional dependence upon his mother and become independent. Or the chaplain could, through the use of interpretation explain all this to the mother and advise her to return home and encourage her son to become a man, which he was trying to do, instead of remaining a little boy. If interpretation were used the mother might reject the chaplain's explanation and refuse to follow his advice because she herself is emotionally dependent and could not, simply by having her problem pointed out to her, accept the proper responsibility for working it out. In using *active-listening* to deal with the same problem the mother would discover the way herself although she would never see far ahead at any given time, therefore she would not be so apt to turn back from the suffering such an effort involves. Further, she would have the companionship and aid of the pastor in her efforts.

Despite the above dangers of rejection by the mother of the chaplain's interpretation, that is the method he used of necessity, for he had but one conference with her, after he reached his analysis of the problem, before she returned home. Through her suffering and through her early conference with the chaplain the mother already had made certain emotional gains, so that she was able to accept the interpretation. Spiritual therapy was being carried on even before the chaplain was certain what the underlying problem was. That is why interpretation is a part of the listening ministry.

D. REASSURANCE

The fourth phase of the *listening* method is reassurance. This method is so different from the first two types of listening that I have frequently described it as a separate method entirely and yet, like interpretation, apart from listening it has little legitimate use. Of the four phases of listening it is least effective and yet of all methods it is used most by clergymen and physicians.

Reassurance is a positive statement by the pastor. It is an expressed opinion that a problem will work itself out or that the pastor believes a parishioner will be able to overcome his suffering. Reassurance is encouragement. The limitation of re-

assurance is not in its desirability but in our failure to bring
the encouragement desired when we reassure people. A person
will not have courage because we tell him to but he can be
helped to develop courage through our listening to him, through
our interest in him and through our own courage. Then we
can tell him he has courage as *we observe he has taken heart
again:* that is reassurance.

As a method, reassurance should be used sparingly. It must
be expressed simply if it is to be effective. The more words
used while reassuring a person the weaker becomes the statement. Small words are the strong words; in attempting to reassure a person use simple terms and be certain that your voice
and manner reveal that you mean them.

Reassurance, for the Protestant, is what the statement of
absolution is for the Catholic, psychologically. "I absolve you
in the name of the Father and the Son and the Holy Ghost,"
is the Catholic statement following confession. The statement
of reassurance is, "I believe you will be all right"; "I can see
a lot of hope in your case"; "I have faith this will not throw
you." "There is no such thing as being ruined except as you
think you are, and you don't think so in this case"; "I believe
in you and I'm going to see you through." A soul-companion
never condemns, never judges, but always attempts to aid.

You will note in the above statements of reassurance that the
Catholic absolution is pronounced in the name of the Trinity,
while the Protestant reassurance is pronounced in the name of
the pastor and personalized around him. This is an advantage
in that it is intimate and personal; it is a disadvantage in that
it is human and thought of as human by the parishioner. The
Protestant's reassurance is limited in that it lacks the perspective, the far view, the support of the Creator Himself.

In our book, *The Art of Ministering to the Sick,* Dr. Cabot
wrote a chapter, that is often accredited to me, entitled, *The*

Two Must Face a Third; namely the parishioner and pastor must face God. I agree. I also recognize that, because of the lack of belief in God of many of our people, it is impossible to face the Third. Many of our clergy in their attempt to be helpful wander off into pious platitudes, only to have their reassurance fail. Two can face God when both know God; when one knows God the other may gradually come to know Him but it is a slow process and not brought about through an easy statement or exhortation. It is brought about through the slow, persistent, affectionate demonstration of the nature of God.

If I were told I could have but one method in pastoral work I would choose the *listening* method. Let us illustrate it further in its various phases through examples taken from actual pastoral work. These illustrations are authentic and are reported by various pastors. Note that most pastors use all four phases of the listening method in a single pastoral conference.

CHAPTER XII

LISTENING CONTINUED

A. Fear

H. M. is twenty years of age. He was arrested for the murder of a cab driver. I had known him when we were boys but have not seen him in recent years. The call was made at the request of his mother. At the time I called he was in jail in a near-by town where he was waiting to be taken back to the state in which the crime was committed. After getting permission from the sheriff to see him and being thoroughly searched I was permitted to enter his cell. The sheriff told me that I would not be required to relate any of our conversation unless he tried to send a message to someone.

Author's Comment	*The Call*
	The sheriff broke the ice by saying, "Someone to see you."
	"Hello, H.," I began. "I don't know whether you remember me or not. I am —— —— who used to live across the street from you."
	"No, I don't remember you."
	"Well, you were only seven. I was ten."
	"Oh yes, I remember you. (Pause) But I thought your name was Jack."
	"No, Jack was my brother.

He used to go with your older sister some. That may be the reason you remember his name."

"Yes, I remember. What are you doing here?" he asks.

"I am going to school over at Dallas. Your mother wrote and asked me to come to see you." Here he looks down at the floor.

He said, "She must be taking it pretty hard. I suppose you know why I am here."

"Yes, I know."

"Did Mother tell you?"

"She didn't say why you were here, but she assumed that I knew. I read about it in the paper."

(a) He immediately becomes defensive. The fact that he is the aggressor in introducing the subject of murder and that he does it so early in the call indicates how much stress he is under.

The minister is the first friendly caller he has had since his arrest so that we expect the call to be significant.

(a) "Well, how does it feel to be talking to a murderer?" His voice was tense as he spoke.

(Frankly, I didn't know where to go from here.)

(b) This is a good answer. It is an effort to reassure the boy.

(b) "Well, H., it is hard to think of you like that. I don't know the details. All I know is what I have read in the paper, and papers are sometimes very unkind in what they say."

(c) Again, this reveals his defensive attitude.

(c) "And I suppose you have come to find out something you

(d) Observe the further effort on the part of the minister to be reassuring.

(e) This is an aggressive question and one that I would criticize the caller for. H. M. has indicated his desire not to be pushed upon the subject of his act.

I would have asked him, "How long have you been here? How have they treated you?" thus giving him a chance to talk about something else, yet letting him carry the conversation in any direction he desires.

(f) The minister is preparing to leave but M. H. does not want him to go as indicated by his questions that follow.

can tell on the witness stand?"

(d) "No, H., I came as a friend to see if I could help you. The sheriff told me that I wouldn't have to repeat anything you told me unless you tried to send a message to someone."

"Well, I'm not talking until I see my lawyer."

"Yes, of course, that is the thing for you to do. When will you go back?" I asked.

"I don't know. Pretty soon, I guess. I signed some papers that I wouldn't fight going back."

(e) "Are you going to plead guilty?"

"I would rather not say."

(f) "That is your privilege, of course. I am in school over at SMU. If there is anything I can do for you before you go back, call me and I will be glad to help you in any way that I can. You surely do have a swell mother and father, H., and I think a lot of your grandmother, too. Your folks wanted someone to come by to see you, and of course, when they wrote me I was only too glad to come."

"What are you studying for over there?"

"I am in the School of Theology."

"What is that?"

"I am going to be a minister."

"Oh, a preacher. Well, I'm not surprised. Your mother was awful religious."

(g) This was done excellently. The statement was accepted simply and then turned back.

(g) "Yes, mother was. Your mother and father are, too, aren't they?"

"Mother is. The old man stays drunk most of the time. He got laid off at the factory since they can't get steel any more, and he couldn't find anything else, so he got started drinking."

(Tears came into his eyes, and I groped for something to say, but he continued):

"I had been drinking too when I killed S. I wouldn't have done it if I hadn't been drinking. He charged me too much for my cab fare and I just got mad and killed him. Do you know him?"

"Yes, he lived just two blocks from me," I replied. "He and his mother lived alone."

"Have you seen her since it happened?"

"No. You see, I have been here in Texas since September."

(h) "I wish I hadn't done it, but I can't undo it now. What would you do?"

(h) This is the crucial point of the call. The pastor needs to draw his attitude out further as the conversation has now moved definitely into the area of religion, which deals with repentance. We are not sure whether he is sorry for the act or sorry because he is in trouble. This could be done through the question, "What do you mean, you wish you hadn't done it?" or, "I don't know what I would do, what have you thought about doing?" This second question moves away from the earlier point which is more significant than the later.

(i) This is about as poorly done as it could be. It is direct advice, it is smug, it is cruel, it is self-righteous.

(i) "Well, H., if I were you I would plead guilty, tell the court I had been drinking, and let them decide. Then whatever their decision, go through with it. (He was crying now.) You see, H., you have committed a great crime. It can't be undone, but you can change your life. Why don't you ask God to forgive you? Why don't you ask the mother of S. to forgive you and take whatever may come?"

"But suppose they electrocute me?"

(j) Argument, judgment!

(j) "That is possible. But you took a life, didn't you? (Pause) The law says you have to pay for a life with a life. However, the court may have mercy on you."

"I am not going to do it. I am not going to plead guilty. I would be crazy if I did."

(k) This adds fuel to the fire. It is arguing; it further suggests a course of action which might not work out as the minister suggests. The court might not have mercy upon him.

(l) This is risky business.

(k) "I don't think so, H. You probably will be proven guilty anyway. If you plead innocent, and they prove you guilty, you *will* get the chair, but if you plead guilty, the court usually gives life instead. (l) Do you mind if I suggest a lawyer?"

"Who?"

"G. C. H. He is a better lawyer, and he will take a greater interest in you than the other. He is also a good friend of mine. If you like I will write him a letter and ask him to see you. Would you like me to?"

"I guess so. Do you think he can help me?"

"He will do all he can. What church do you belong to?"

"C—— Church."

"I would also get Brother F. to come to see me, if I were you." (Brother F. is the pastor of the church.)

"I don't like him."

"Well, would you like me to
write my pastor and ask him to
see you? He would be glad to,
and he will be able to help you
more than I could."

"Yes, I would."

The jailer had been pacing up
and down in front of the cell for
some time, so I thought I ought
to go. I suggested prayer, and
prayed a short prayer. Then I
left.

Author's Summary

The condition of this call is unusual for the average clergyman but the details are not. The problem of helping to relieve
tension and searching out a person's mind who is in difficulty
is our constant task. Just what the basic attitude of this boy
was we do not know. Again, it is the old question, "How do
you feel about it?" Religion is not limited by the fact that a
man has committed murder.

So far as his method was concerned this call reveals the ex-
tremes of good and bad method; the early phases of a hard
situation were handled well but the minister missed his opportunity at (h) and then all was lost.

The call did harm, I would say.

B. FEAR AND GUILT

MR. H. T.

Mr. T. is thirty-eight years old. He married quite young
and has a family of four children, the youngest of whom is
six years old and the oldest is seventeen. Mr. T. is well groomed,
educated, has a stable job, and is enthusiastically religious. At

the close of a morning service, where the Lord's Supper had been administered, he spoke to me, as he was leaving the church.

Author's Comment	First Call
	"I would like to see you sometime, when you have the time, preacher," said Mr. T.
(a) It is desirable to arrange to see a parishioner following such a request as soon as possible.	(a) "I would be happy to see you, Mr. T. any time. If you will give me about five minutes, I will be in my study, if you want to come now." Mr. T. replied, "Well, then I'll wait." After finishing greeting those who were waiting, I went to the study.
(b) Good observation—indicates stress.	(b) Mr. T. was standing, although several chairs were in the room.
	"I want to quit the church, and move to another," were Mr. T.'s first words upon my entering.
(c) He wanted to be certain the pastor observed his failure to participate in the Communion Service.	(c) "I suppose that you noticed that I did not partake of the Lord's Supper, this morning."
	"Yes," I replied, "I did notice it, Mr. T." Whereupon I waited for his reply, which came suddenly, "I don't think that the people here appreciate me or even understand me."
(d) Good method, the pastor agrees but passes it back to the parishioner.	(d) "That's possible but what do you mean?"
	"I mean that I don't believe like these people, and that I can't

take the Lord's Supper, because I am not 'in love and harmony' with my fellow man, not even some of those who parade up to the altar."

(e) Poor method, he accepts the discussion of the communion at face value instead of considering it a symptom. Better to have answered, "What do you mean, 'not in love and harmony'?"

(e) "Well, Mr. T., I have ⑤ always believed that the Lord's Supper was a sort of individual affair, that is, at that time I don't consider the other person or his beliefs, but turn inwardly and observe my own shortcomings, and ask for forgiveness."

(f) In spite of the pastor's poor method more material was revealed.

(f) "Well, I suppose that is what we all should do but then, you see, I have had trouble in my family in Colorado." Here Mr. T. began to relate his life history and tell of experiences during his boyhood days at home on the farm. He ended by saying, "You know it's funny how you can love someone like your mother or brother, until they have cheated you out of something and then you just quit."

(g) Good.

(g) "What do you mean, Mr. ⑥ T., that you just quit?"

"Well, last month, my mother divided up the farm, and gave all of the other children their share except me. She gave my share to my brother."

"I see," I replied.

"Then I went to see a lawyer about it and we had the case in court. My mother insisted that I had a good job, and didn't need the land. I do have a good job but believe that I should have had my share. Anyway the court awarded it to my brother. Do you think that they treated me fairly?"

(h) Mistake in method. The pastor opposes Mr. T. Better to have said, "It would seem that was unfair. Why do you think your mother did that?" He has just told the pastor why but I would try to get him to go over it again from his own angle.

(h) I replied, "At times, Mr. T., I am afraid that our sense of fairness is greatly limited."

(i) When the pastor opposes him he leaves.
Summary: This conference is unsatisfactory due to the poor technique of the pastor.

(i) "Well, I guess that's right, but it's way past noon, and I won't keep you longer—thanks for helping me."

Second Call

(a) Fortunately, the pastor can make a follow-up call when he recognizes stress. The minister seems to have failed to recognize the parishioner's statement that leaving the church was a symptom of some deeper need.

(a) I called on Mr. T. after working hours at his home, hoping to find why he desired to leave the membership of the church. As I entered the room, Mr. T. was seated by the radio. I was shown in by Mrs. T., his wife, who also had been an active member in the church until a few weeks preceding this call.

(b) This is a good general question but he uses it too soon.

(b) "Hello, Mr. T., how are things going?" to which he responded, "Fine," and invited me to sit down. Whereupon he began to relate the important events of his day at the office.

(c) Good observation.

(c) Mrs. T. was also seated with us and bore evidence of being embarrassed. In a few minutes, she excused herself, leaving Mr. T. and myself alone.

(d) The parishioner introduces their former conversation which indicates continued stress. The latter part of his statement is like his threat to leave the church; it is an effort to gain the pastor's interest through "shock statements."

(d) "I've been thinking of our conversation of last Sunday," began Mr. T. "I suppose that you think I am very odd."

(e) Good reassurance.

(e) "No, I don't think that you are odd, for after all we all have our striking differences."

"Well, you know we have a fellow down at the office who is almost forty, and has his family already well started. Now at his age, he and his wife are going to have another child, and he seems quite pleased over it."

Here I grunted and asked, "Well, that's part of life, isn't it?"

"Well, I don't know. I don't think that a man and his wife should have children when they already have a family, to me it seems almost indecent."

(f) Excellent.

(f) "Why do you think that it's indecent?" I asked.

"Well, to me it would certainly be a sin to have people say that the T.'s are having another child. I believe that if we were, I'd be almost tempted to move away from here, so people wouldn't know it."

(g) Good follow-up.

(g) "Do you believe that would eliminate your present feeling about it?" I asked.

"It would at least keep people from laughing and talking, wouldn't it?"

"I suppose that it would, but then I really don't know anyone who would consider the matter as laughable, do you?"

"No, I suppose I don't but there would be some who would talk behind your back about it."

(h) Perhaps reassurance was needed here, but it would seem to have continued with the method of *directed listening* would have been better, as "Why do you think people would laugh? Having children is perfectly natural."

(h) "To me the matter of having children is simply an ordinary process through which most married people go, and the matter of childbirth is so common that people today accept it without embarrassment or at least to me they should."

"Yes, but it's hard to believe all of that."

(i) This little question is the most aggressive and often the most fruitful of any we ask.

(i) "Why?" I asked.

"Well, it is because there are people like me who are old fashioned, I guess." There entered here a long discourse between the modern ways, and old fashioned ways of doing things. He ended this by giving his wife's recent poor health as an excuse for doing less work in the church. I asked, "Have you had Mrs. T. to the clinic?"

"Well, yes, but we are not sure what's wrong with her." Here I waited saying nothing. "It could be heart trouble, or something else, you know how these doctors are.

(j) Now the above conversation begins to fit together.

(j) "We changed doctors last week, for he thought that she was pregnant, but I know that's wrong. However, this new doctor hasn't said what he thinks."

(k) Again, reassurance. Even here the pastor could have gone back into underlying attitudes.

(k) "Well, if it is that, then I offer my congratulations, and should be very glad to call on your wife during her confinement."

(l) It is always possible to keep such an event to yourself, of course!

(l) "You know this thing has had me worried, but we hope to keep it to ourselves, if it does prove to be a child."

(m) Further reassurance.

(m) "Well, I am sure, Mr. T., that all of your friends will be quite pleased and happy for you to have a new member in your home."

"Yes, I guess that they will."

(n) This was well done; he just ignores the threat to "quit the church" which was correct. Mr. T. does not want to leave the church, he just wanted some help

(n) "By the way, Mr. T., I have here some plans for our Memorial Day service at the church, and since you are chairman of this special committee I

from his pastor, which he received.

wanted you to revise and direct them."

"Many thanks, I will do the best I can."

"I'll see you Wednesday night, then?"

"Yes, if nothing prevents my attending."

"Good night, Mr. T."

(o) This would indicate the call was effective and helpful.

(o) "Good night, Brother E, and many thanks for getting me over my worry, hurry back to see us again."

Pastor's Summary

There were many things that I knew about this case before it came to me. I already knew that both doctors had examined Mrs. T. and that she was to have a baby. I knew also about the trouble in the family over the land for that was an old settled matter. So when Mr. T. talked of this trouble to cover up the fact that there was to be an addition to his family, I began to work on the theory of both guilt and fear. At times I refused to follow my leads, and argued. However, now four weeks after these calls the T.'s are attending church, the wife is active as ever, and he seems in high spirits.

Author's Summary

The test of a call is, does it help? Mr. T. was helped, therefore the pastor's work was effective. At the same time we see faulty method used and little underlying insight gained for the parishioner. We can but speculate about the relationship of the feelings revealed.

Mr. and Mrs. T. have four children, they had decided not to

have any more, but being "old fashioned" as Mr. T. described them, they do nothing to prevent having others, they probably know nothing to do. He has had trouble with his family over his inheritance, which he feels he needs to support his already large family. To be treated thus by his mother was a blow, then the universe deals him another blow through his wife's becoming pregnant again. He needs to talk to someone and he needs reassurance. His pastor accepts his story, is not surprised or condemnatory. Release from his stress is gained through talking about it. While the pastor's method was at fault the calls were helpful. *Directed listening* was indicated and necessary. The problem was fear and guilt, with overtones of resentment which stemmed from the other two emotions.

C. Guilt and Loneliness

Mrs. L. R.

The young daughter of Mrs. R. had joined the church two weeks previous to this call. The call was intended to make the acquaintance of the child's mother. Mrs. R. was an attractive woman about the age of thirty-five. She appeared to be in good physical health. The nice apartment gave evidence of much care and good financial support.

Author's Comment	*The Call*
	I rang the bell for the upper apartment and stepped inside the door. In just a moment Mrs. R. came to the head of the stairs; she had a worried expression on her face. She called, "Won't you come up?"
	"Thank you, I will."

She turned and walked back into the apartment before I could reach the top of the stairs.

(a) Here we have a situation of exaggerated stress.

(a) Just as I entered the room she turned suddenly and burst into tears.

I said, "I hope I haven't disturbed you."

"No, you are just in time." She was still crying aloud.

"Yes?"

"I was just on my knees praying for the first time since I was a little girl."

(b) This is a statement of encouragement and reassurance.

(b) "I am glad I came just at this time if I can be of any help to you." I handed her my card.

She said, "My mind has never been so jumbled up. I feel that you can help me."

In the adjoining room I saw a pint of whiskey open on the table.

(c) Further encouragement. Well done.

(c) I said, "We are all confused at times and feel like we need to talk to someone."

We both seated ourselves on the divan. I turned slightly to the side so I could face her.

She said, "I suppose you have smelled the whiskey by now?"

"Yes."

"I had to do something."

(d) This is good *directed listening*. He takes her back to her earlier statement.

(d) "You told me that you were praying when I arrived."

Her crying had ceased but she continued to dry her eyes. "Yes,

I was praying and asking God to help me. It seems as if he sent you here. I am not such a good church worker now but I used to be. I try to keep my two daughters going to church all the time. I have wanted to join your church with them but have felt that the people wouldn't understand me." (Pause)

(e) Good question.

(e) "Have you ever joined a church?"

(f) Indication of guilt feelings, but the pastor must let them reveal themselves as they will.

(f) "Yes, and that is why the people wouldn't understand me. I don't want to move my letter, I want to join all over again. Can a person do that?"

"Yes, if you desire." (Pause)

(g) Now he begins his search —note that his method is *directed listening*.

(g) I said, "Your daughter gave N. as her last name, is Mr. N. living?"

"Yes, we were divorced over a year ago. My two daughters are by him. He is in San Francisco and sends a good sum of money to keep them in school and take care of their every need."

"Does Mr. R. work in Chicago?"

"No, he travels most of the time." (Pause) She said, "He is such a nice person. He loves us three so much and does everything possible to make us happy. My two girls seem to be very happy. (h) I don't deserve him."

(h) More indication of guilt feelings.

(i) Good follow-up.

(i) "Why do you say that?"

"I feel so guilty."

"Yes?"

"I just got a phone call from the doctor. I am going to have a baby."

(j) This is the first point I would criticize in the pastor's technique. He makes this mistake by blindly assuming that all people are happy over having babies. Better to have said, "Why has that disturbed you?"

(j) "I am sure Mr. R. will be proud."

"Yes, he will. I don't deserve him or the baby."

(k) This is better.

(k) "Why do you say that?"

(l) Here the story comes with its revelation of frustration, disappointment and guilt feelings.

(l) "My first husband was not good for me; he drank and ran around too much. I warned him that I would divorce him but waited a long time before I did. I have tried to forget him and can't. He doesn't know it but in spite of the fact that he was mean to me, he took a place in my life that can't be replaced. Mr. R. is perfect but even his kindness won't wipe out memories. I feel that it is unfair for me to have his baby as long as I feel as I do. Every time that Mr. R. and I have done the sex act I have felt guilty. I do him wrong each time. He acts as if he doesn't know anything is wrong but I know he must be able to tell."

(m) Here I would criticize the pastor severely. His statement of

(m) I said, "The first love is always very strong but we must

reassurance comes too quickly and easily. I always test a confession to see if it is complete through asking further questions, as "Have you felt this way ever since you married Mr. R.?"

(n) However, her willingness to accept the reassurance is an indication that the confession was complete.

(o) This is her statement of reassurance, and would indicate she was free from the guilt. The rest of the call tapers off. Had they not been interrupted it should have closed with prayer.

The pastor should have followed up this call with another the following week, not waiting for her to call of her own accord.

sometimes forget it. Your feelings are natural. I feel that your primary concern is to prepare for the baby's happiness."

(n) "Yes, the baby will have a life to live and I should make it happy. I had let that slip my mind."

"Children bring much happiness, don't they?"

(o) "Yes, they do. Maybe this child will help me to forget the past and be happier with Mr. R."

"I am sure it will."

"I'll have to forget the whiskey from now on."

"It would be best."

"Isn't it strange that the first time I prayed in years seemed to bring me some help?"

"It seems to be a wonderful thing."

The younger daughter enters from school.

Mrs. R. said, "F., this is Mr. ——."

Daughter: "Yes, I know. How are you?"

"Fine, and you are too, I hope."

Daughter: "Yes, I am. I like Blank Church."

"I'm very glad."

Mrs. R.'s best friend came in and we were introduced.

"I must go, I am sure you have plans."

Mrs. R. followed me to the door.

I said, "I hope I can see you again soon. If I can be of any help feel free to call me."

She said, "I feel much better now. Come back when you can."

"Thank you, I will. Goodbye."

"Goodbye."

Mrs. R. phoned the office a few days later and asked about the technical points of joining the church again. She seemed in good spirits. The second Sunday following the call she came forward to be baptised. She seemed very much unafraid of the people about.

Author's Comment

This opportunity would not have come to the pastor of its own accord. He was able to help her because he was the first person Mrs. R. talked to after talking with her physician.

Her problem was guilt and loneliness—loneliness for her former husband.

CHAPTER XIII

PRAYER

A WOMAN told me of her feeling of "aloneness." She could not pray, she said, and feel any warmth of fellowship in her prayer although she has always been a devoted mother and an active church member. At the time she told me the story she was in a state of nervous and physical exhaustion. A son and daughter had died five years before. When I inquired how long she had felt this barrenness in her devotional life she began to speak of a tragedy which had happened sixteen years ago when a car her son was driving turned over and killed the young daughter of a clergyman. Despite the son's efforts to alleviate the family's suffering the minister had felt deep resentment and had threatened to kill the lad. Since that time she had not been able to pray with any degree of satisfaction.

In time of personal crisis many people lose their way religiously and, having lost their way, their personal crisis deepens, for they have nothing to support them. Most people take their faith for granted and go along fairly well until something happens to them. Then they cannot pray effectively. They cannot pray because they do not really believe in God, or understand the purpose of prayer. All too often God is thought of as a glorified errand boy, who cometh when we say come and goeth when we say go.

Prayer is man's effort to release resources in his behalf which are beyond his own control. The basic question concerning prayer is, does it help? Does it release new resources? Does prayer increase God's interest in us and our struggles? Here is a child who is dying and the parents request the pastor's prayers; here is a man facing life with a handicap and the pastor comes to pray with him; here is a girl whose heart is broken because of a frustrated love affair; here is a person who is ill, another who thinks his life is a failure; here is a man who feels guilty; here is a woman who is lonely; here is a soldier or sailor in danger. Will prayer help? Will they find in prayer the answer to their needs?

Prayer will help; but it may not help in the specific way that is intended by the supplicant.

Will prayer change God's Mind? *It will not.*

God's Mind does not need to be changed. It is Sufficient and Creative. Prayer changes our own minds. It brings us into close touch with the Creative Mind of God and strengthens us. Many a person dies who prays for health and many a person is hurt who prays for safety. But the person who prays for health honestly and in humility, assists the health-giving resources already within his body which is God at work. The person who prays for safety is conscious of danger and therefore is more alert and wisely cautious than another.

Prayer, especially the prayer which is prayed by one standing beside us who is free from the heat of the suffering, reminds us of the things we have forgotten and causes us to relax our desires into Greater Desires than our own. It helps us to gain perspective and see that the limited vision we have of ourselves is not the whole of our living. Prayer helps us to trust the world in which we live; to trust the people about us, the chairs upon which we sit, the ground upon which we walk, the day with its work and the night that gives us rest. Especially it helps us as we see other trusting people who pray.

When all this is said and done there is still much of mystery in prayer.

I was told of an American soldier in Australia who had a

moronic urge to kill civilian women. After the third murder he was apprehended. When he was brought before the military authorities he said, "That's what I was sent over here for. To kill people!" When it was pointed out that he was not sent to Australia to kill civilian women but Japanese soldiers he failed to see the point. He was tried and sentenced to be hanged. The chaplain saw him regularly, ministering to him up to and including the time of his execution. When it was over the chaplain said to his superior officer, "When I die, I hope I'll go to as happy a heaven as that man went to." There is Christian faith! There is the mystery of religion, the mystery of God's redeeming power that may be released through prayer.

Prayer fails when we attempt to bend the powers of the universe to our desires; it helps when we bring ourselves into line with its creative forces. The pastor will do well not to use the phrase, "Thy will be done," in his pastoral work. This phrase probably is the most misunderstood one in the whole New Testament. If we pray, "Thy will be done" with a sick person he is apt to think we are asking God not to spare him; when we pray, "Thy will be done" with a person who is sick and he dies, the family is sure God killed him and they rather think we had a part in it; while if we pray, "Thy will be done" with a broken-hearted girl she is certain to think God did not approve of her love. There are other ways of bringing a parishioner into touch with God through prayer than through using this phrase.

A further objection to it is that people are constantly dying when it is not God's will, otherwise why the tremendous resources for health, for happiness, for affection and friendliness which are within us? To believe it is God's will that we suffer because we have sinned is a false assumption. Suffering is an instrument of God for creative growth, not an end in itself for punishment. It often is the pastor's task to interpret suffering to the sufferer; to help him discover how suffering may be turned into triumphant living even as our Lord turned suffering into victory.

In his use of prayer in pastoral work the minister should always strive for quietness within himself. This is best achieved through physical relaxation as suggested in chapter X. Thus the same condition is suggested to the parishioner. The tone of voice should be modulated, easy, natural. Why so many of our clergy feel they must pray in a pious, other-worldly tone is incomprehensible; one wonders if they think God does not understand a quiet, natural voice. This tendency grows out of a desire to suggest awe through the voice; it suggests spiritual nausea rather than awe to most sensible people. Naturalness, ease, dignity, quietness are the characterization of effective pastoral prayer.

The prayer should never be long—about the number of phrases that are contained in the twenty-third Psalm will be long enough. It is surprising how we come to have a feel for the length of a prayer as well as for its content when we ourselves are in a prayerful mood.

Prayer in a Home

Eternal God, Father of us all;
Thou who hast blessed us through love and affection,
We give Thee thanks for homes and the joys of home;
We give Thee thanks for these Thy children;
Continue to bless them and make them strong in faith.
Bless the husband and father, the wife and mother
Of this home. Through their love for each other
May they know Thy love for them.
Bless the son and daughter of this home, and
May they know the joys of men and women as they know the joys
    of youth.

We pray for homes less fortunate;
May we be mindful of our neighbors and serve them as they have
 served us.
We pray for the church, family of families, and home of homes,
United in love for Thee, through Jesus Christ, our Lord. AMEN.

Prayer of Thanksgiving upon the Birth of a Child

Almighty and Everloving Father, Creator and Sustainer of life,
We give Thee thanks for the joys of living, and for the strength of
 health,
For the safe care of this one, we thank Thee,
We rejoice in the affection of this mother and father,
New life from their lives, new strength and faith and hope;
Bless this child, O God, and make it Thine own.
We remember that our Lord came into the world as a child,
We know the joy His mother knew as she held Him in her arms.
As we share the mother's joy so we know the father's hope;
Strengthen this mother and father in their parenthood,
And may their affection overflow into this new life;
Grant them health and faith for the day's task, through Jesus Christ,
 our Lord. AMEN.

Prayer for One Who Is Ill

Eternal Father, Who art near unto us at all times,
We give Thee thanks for the gift of life and the strength of faith;
In hard moments we turn to Thee, in lonely moments Thou art our
 companion;
We thank Thee for doctors and nurses, and all who seek to bring us
 health,
We remember our loved ones, strengthen them and keep them safe.
Bless this one, give him quietness of soul and ease from pain,
And make strong the forces of health within him;
May he know the support of the Everlasting Arms
And the confidence of the Everlasting Hope.
In the name of Christ, we pray. AMEN.

Prayer for a Bereaved Family

Lord and Father of us all,
We give Thee thanks for life and the joys of life,
We give Thee thanks for faith and the hope of faith.
Thou hast taught us to love Thee through Thy love for us,
We rest in Thee.
In this hour we rest in Thy support,
And we know the strength of the Everlasting Arms——
We rest our loved one in Thee.
That one who is near unto us in affection,
Now is with Thee; may we gain comfort from the thought.
Strengthen this family, the mother, these children,
And may they find comfort in Thee.
May we remember it is but a short time
Until we too will pass along this way to be reunited with our loved
    ones.
We pray in the name of Jesus Christ, our Lord. AMEN.

Prayer for a Soldier Son

Heavenly Father, Lord of the nations, Thou who hast blessed us with
    faith and hope,
We pray for the son of this home who serves his nation,
Through our prayers we commune with him;
Bless him and make him strong for the day's task,
And bring him home again, strong in faith.
We pray for our nation and for all who serve Thee through serving it.
We repent of our sins and selfishness, and
We dedicate ourselves to the high task of serving our fellow men,
That wars may cease and righteousness abound among the nations,
In the name of Jesus Christ, our Lord. AMEN.

CHAPTER XIV

RECORDS

THE pastor has not usually kept records of his pastoral work and personal counseling. This has been because of the confidential nature of his work, on the one hand, and his failure to understand the importance of records, on the other. The fact that he has not kept records is responsible, more than any other single thing, for the pastor's failure to develop a discipline equal to other professional workers in the humanitarian field. It is not enough to say he did not have the knowledge; if records had been kept the knowledge would have been forthcoming and the physician would now be turning to the clergyman for understanding, instead of the amazing situation of the pastor turning to the physician for understanding of the spiritual problems of his own people. It is not that the physician disagrees with the pastor—he simply ignores him. It has not occurred to the physician that the pastor has much to contribute to the individual's welfare. The great difference between the two professions is that the physician is studying his failures, keeping records of them, and publishing his observations, so that other members of the profession may learn from those failures.

There are several types of pastoral records. One is the complete, detailed, verbatim record such as we have been using in our clinical training for ten years, as found in chapter XII. This is a study record. It is written so that the minister may study it and examine the problems which were revealed during the call but which he, and sometimes the parishioner, were not conscious of because of the emotional pressures which were involved in the call. Studying the record calmly, often studying two or three calls upon the same person at one time, the pastor may discover an underlying pattern of thought which he had not recognized before.

Our literature and progress in the field of pastoral work will be based upon this type of record. It is interesting that such a record will reveal spiritual needs and faulty methods which the pastor in making the call and writing the records was not conscious of. It is through the use of such records that we will carry on our instruction and improve our effectiveness.

There is a second type of record which is a summary of a call with little or no direct quotation listed; here each call is listed and new material is especially noted. This is a work record and is apt to reveal facts more than it reveals emotions and underlying problems. It is useful to the pastor largely in recalling topics which have been discussed with a given parishioner. It is not apt to reveal problems except as the pastor is conscious of them at the time of the conference. A pastor who is carrying a large burden of work, and who is skilled in recognizing emotions and emotional attitudes in relation to subjects discussed, will be able to use this type of record effectively. This record is not particularly useful for study purposes and contributes to knowledge only insofar as a large series of problems are studied in an effort to discover spiritual needs.

The third type of record is simply a listing of the persons called upon or counseled with and the date of the contact, with no indication of what took place during the conference. This record is useful as a check upon himself by the pastor in his pastoral work. It shows how little or how much pastoral work has been done. The pastor who reports he has made over two hundred calls in a month, has preached four to eight sermons, attended fifteen committee meetings and given six other talks before various groups, has little conception of pastoral work. Furthermore, a person who is so emotionally unstable as to have to work that hard is one to be distrusted. The hospital chaplain who makes thirty calls or more a day is doing ineffective work. Listing one's calls reveals the type of work we are doing.

Another advantage of this type of record is that it prevents the forgetting of certain parishioners all clergymen would like to forget. There are always such people in every parish. Dr. Henry Sloane Coffin has said, "The Lord will see to it that in every parish you will find a certain number of disagreeable people." If you forget these lords and ladies, when they are sick, or in your routine calling, you will not have helped your ministry nor your soul's confidence. A little attention sometimes does wonders for a disagreeable person.

The careful minister will use all three of these types of records for he will have people with varying degrees of needs.

PART FIVE

PASTORAL WORK AND THE CHURCH

CHAPTER XV

PREACHING AND PASTORAL WORK

MOST clergymen think of themselves as called "to preach" and they give a major amount of their time and energy to the task of preaching. A certain amount of it is sheer exhibitionism. In fact, preaching is ineffective unless the preacher has considerable ability to portray through his voice and personality the truth he is setting forth. The radio and the movie house have cut down his drawing power as an interesting public speaker and he may expect the cut to be even greater in the future.

Preaching as the principal method of carrying on the work of the church is rapidly declining. Those communions that have emphasized preaching and have been indifferent to other phases of the church's program are failing to hold their membership while other churches go steadily forward. The Church of the Latter Day Saints (Mormon) is one of the most rapidly growing religious groups in America. Every family belonging to the Mormon church is called upon every month by the elders (clergy) for the specific purpose of inquiring into the spiritual condition of that family. It is interesting that the Mormons were the only major religious group to take their members off the relief rolls during the depression of the twenties. The Southern Baptists, another rapidly growing denomination, have a strong religious educational program plus a constant emphasis upon personal evangelism, both of which contain the essence of fellowship as described in chapter IX. The Episcopal Church, where preaching is not recognized as its greatest strength but where worship is emphasized, is a steadily growing communion and one that is holding its membership. In the Lutheran Church we find the happy combination of preaching, pastoral work, education and worship; it also is a steadily growing communion. One test of a communion is not whether it recruits new members but whether it holds its old members.

Dr. Henry Sloane Coffin is fond of saying that it was not preaching but the "ringing of door bells" that built the great Madison Avenue Presbyterian Church in New York City which reached such heights of popularity during his pastorate there. But let no one be misled, Henry Sloane Coffin never neglected his preaching, and through the years he has given a major amount of attention to teaching the art of preaching to young ministers. While he has taught pastoral work he has never written upon the subject, much to the loss of American Protestantism.

It is not uncommon to find a minister who is described as a "weak" preacher but who is serving as pastor of an active and growing congregation. When examined carefully such a clergyman almost inevitably is found to have served that church for some years, during which time he has emphasized pastoral work. *His people love him.* The simple truths which he points out in his sermons are personal in their meaning to his listeners for he has been in their homes, stood beside their sick beds, rejoiced with them in good fortune and suffered with them in sorrow. He has baptized their babies, married their young people and buried their dead. But he has done more than conduct the formal services these functions require. He has known when a young mother was apprehensive, he has held homes steady when ship-wreck was threatened, he has brought affection to the aged and comforted the bereaved. His sermons hold truths for his people because he knows their needs and has known where to find the truths for those needs from the storehouse of religion. His preaching is effective because it helps people with the job of living, which is the acid test of preaching.

The preacher who draws his sermons from his own thought and from books but does not go about among his people, who never gives them an opportunity to tell him their thoughts, may have perfected the academic art of preaching but he will fail as a preacher. It is like the physician who has mastered the subject of anatomy from the study of cadavers but has never studied disease in living bodies.

A preacher always preaches about his own problems, it cannot be otherwise for such is the "growing edge" of his life. If he is a pastor his problems are his people's problems, therefore his sermons are realistic and, in so far as he knows the resources of religion, he is helpful in his preaching. The preacher's task is to bring into the lives of his people the Eternal Truths.

The clergyman who knows human problems but does not know Eternal Truth, God and the Ways of God, fails in preaching. He is not a clergyman, he is a psychologist. The psychologist studies the human mind and human behavior; as a psychologist he makes no claim to a knowledge of God or of knowing how to bring God and man into harmony. In actual practice a clinical psychologist often serves as minister in that he does bring God and man together. God works through many, and oftentimes strange, channels.

One of the grave dangers of preaching is that the preacher may overshadow the truth he is talking about. Protestantism is characterized by the message; therefore the messenger is placed in the center of the church facing the people. Because of the frailty of the messenger he may glorify himself rather than God, so that people join the preacher rather than the church. When the preacher leaves that church for another, or for heaven, there is no loyalty that holds them. If the pulpit is placed to one side, if worship through communion, music, prayer and responses takes place, if God is glorified through the beauty of church architecture, if the religious heritage of the ages is present, then the limitations of preaching are overcome. As pointed out elsewhere, pastoral work faces this same danger of glorifying the pastor.

Preaching is clergy-centered; pastoral work is parishioner centered. It is difficult to bring the two together but it is possible. Many who have concentrated upon preaching think of themselves as pastors but they violate the basic practices of good pastoral work, as described in chapter XI, by talking about themselves, giving advice, reassurance, and manipulating their own ideas into the conversation or playing their personalities so that they dominate the parishioner. The role of the preacher is an individualistic one. While preaching, the clergyman is on his own; he makes or breaks that part of the service. It is true that the feeling of rapport between the preacher and the congregation inspires him to greater effort and strength. At the same time a part of the art of preaching is the ability to gain this feeling of friendliness between congregation and preacher. The clergyman who does not have that ability fails in his preaching. Rapport generally rests back upon the pastoral work which has been carried on in the past.

A physician on our hospital staff said recently, "We have a new pastor at our church. I've not been to hear him although he's been there three months. I had a birthday last week, and of all things here came a birthday card from the pastor. Guess I'll have to go round and hear him preach."

A basic function of the pulpit is to carry on a teaching ministry. In this the relationship between pastoral work and preaching is strong and clear. One test of preaching is whether it brings people to the pastor to talk about their problems. The preacher who never has anyone come to see him or request him to call upon them or members of their family is failing and should examine his message and his pastoral work. This may necessitate consulting a counselor, particularly a psychiatric counselor, so that the preacher may gain some understanding of himself and why he is failing. Those preachers who are super-egotists and who are steaming along, attracting attention and having a wonderful time, will never consult a psychiatrist although many times their wives and children find it necessary. Such men not only help few people but they definitely harm the cause of Christ and His Kingdom.

There are many sermons that will grow directly out of pastoral work, although the preacher must be careful of the kinds of illustrations he uses even though the experience took place in an entirely different congregation. The woman sitting in the second row who desires help in a marital situation that is going badly, the man sitting in the back pew who has been drinking because of his inability to turn in the number of orders his sales manager expects, the high school boy sitting in the balcony, will think, "He talks about other people, he makes wise cracks about their troubles, he would talk the same about me." They go away sorrowing. The minister can deal with personal problems without citing illustrations such as, "I met a woman and she said to me ———."

A sermon titled, "The Resources of Religion in Time of Trouble" may deal with faith and the strengths of faith, why doubt comes and how faith is gained and actually strengthened through trouble. Go to the history of Israel for illustrations, go to Jeremiah and Hosea, to the Gospels, to Paul, to John Bunyan; biographical literature is filled with illustration of the triumph of faith in the midst of suffering.

A sermon upon, "The Returning Son and the Forgiving

Father," would develop around the parable of the Prodigal Son, and would be directed toward those suffering from a sense of guilt and failure. Here we see the Mind and Nature of God more clearly than at any other place in the New Testament. Most people are not sinners in the sense that they consistently and persistently work at the job; those people will not be in the church, although their wives might be present. The average person indulges in the minor sins and does not feel his religion is helpful because he is so uncomfortable when he comes to church.

"The Ability to Accept God" would be a sermon that would afford the pastor an opportunity to point out the defensive nature of persons who have known emotional insecurity at home. How can a person love God or permit God to love him who has heard his mother and father quarrel all his life, who has been bullied by his older brother and father and who has never had anyone put his arms around him and say, "I love you, Little Man?"

Ministry to the sick starts in the pulpit, and I am not talking about sick sermons. Our people should be instructed about what to expect from the pastor in time of illness and death. In such a sermon the minister may say simply, "When I call upon you when you are ill we will talk about what you want to talk about. We will tell stories if you desire but you will have to tell the first one. If you want to tell me how you feel about your suffering, your discouragement, your embarrassments, your failures you will have the opportunity to do so. And of this you may be sure: I will listen and be interested in whatever you tell me. And further, whatever you tell me will not be told to another. We know that talking with someone in whom you have confidence, about what is worrying you or what has happened to you, helps you to become free of it emotionally, to get it out of your mind, to conquer it. There is no event so insignificant, no fear so small but that it is important to me, if it is to you. When I call upon you when you are sick we will have prayer if you want us to. The prayer is for you. It is not that your pastor's prayer is to replace yours, or that mine will have more influence with God. Rather it is that I stand free from your suffering. I am able to see life steadily and see it whole which, as a sick person, whose perspective and vision are limited, you cannot. I am able to be calm and relaxed which in itself helps you to permit God to bless you with confidence and calmness, therein aiding you in the recovery of health.

"The same thing is true if you are sick unto death. It is to be hoped that you will have made your peace with God long before you come to die. But dying is a lonely experience, your body is fighting disease, your mind is confused by drugs. Foreign thoughts lay hold upon your mind as bacteria lay hold upon your body. My prayer serves to reassure you, to drive out doubts as medicine drives out disease, to remind you and make real to you again the things you believe but have forgotten.

"Finally, remember: I am as near to you as the telephone, at any hour of the day or night. If you call me I will rejoice in the opportunity you have given me, in the trust you have placed in me, through your asking me to call. We may not solve your problem, but in so far as you are able to seek and accept help, we will strengthen you in your efforts to live with your problem. Try as I will I am not able to know you are sick unless you send me word. You will notify the ice man, the milk man and the paper boy, perhaps you will remember also to notify your pastor when you are ill, and going to the hospital." I venture to suggest that such a sermon will be remembered a long time, especially if it is repeated, in one way or another, about once each year.

The subject of suffering should be much in your sermons;

the Christian conception needs constant interpretation. Vague and negative preaching about evil and sin is largely a waste of time. Your people do not need to be told you are against evil, that they may assume. And to run in the subject of drink as a filler because you have nothing else to say is a sure sign of too many committee meetings and too little pastoral work during the past week. If you desire to deliver a helpful sermon upon the question of drink, which is one of the most serious problems of our time, read one or two modern books upon the subject and deal with it from the standpoint of why people drink.[1]

Preaching as the most effective method of carrying on the work of the Kingdom has turned the corner. The military chaplains' experience in the present war where the significant part of their work is with individuals, even though they were largely untrained for the task, will have a tremendous effect upon the future work of the pastor. This does not mean that great preachers will not arise or that effective preaching will not be done. It does mean that the man who feels he is called upon only to preach should expect to work in some other profession than the ministry.

I have this further feeling, men and women with a fair amount of intelligence can be taught how to avoid doing harm in pastoral work, while no amount of instruction can teach them how to avoid doing harm through preaching. The needs of our people are so great and the Spirit of God is abroad so strongly that even poor mediums may be used in bringing man and God together through pastoral work, while preaching, apart from pastoral work, calls for the genius of a prophet.

[1] *Alcohol: One Man's Meat,* Strecker and Chambers. The Macmillan Company, New York, 1938.

CHAPTER XVI

THE CLERGYMAN AND OTHER
PROFESSIONAL WORKERS

THE physician, the nurse, social worker and clergyman are the four major humanitarian professional workers. Two of these professions are dominated by men and two by women. Because of their emotional make-up women have a difficult time in medicine just as they do in the ministry. There are few men case-workers, although there are many men serving as administrators in social work. There are few men nurses. Women who go into medicine and the ministry usually are masculine in temperament, while men who become social workers and nurses are effeminate in temperament. As a matter of fact men who are physicians and clergyman are more sensitive by nature than are men of other professions; it is this sensitivity that gives them an awareness of human suffering and makes the alleviation of suffering vital to them.

In addition to these four professional groups there are others who give some attention to work with spiritual problems through counseling. The attorney does some work in this field, although the extent and quality of his work is difficult to measure. The consulting psychologist, the college counselor and the occupational therapist are still numerically small and their training and effectiveness vary greatly. Because the group is small not much need be said about them except to point out that such professions do exist and their members are at work in the field of counseling. We may expect both college counseling and occupational therapy programs to increase in the future. The newest development in the humanitarian field is the appearance of the personnel worker in industry. He is a combination of clergyman, psychologist and ward-heeler. His task is not yet clearly defined and his training is not established. In some situations he hires and fires, in others he does not; often he is the bridge between employer and employee; he works with the human side of things and with human problems as they affect the worker and production. His coming marks a new day in industry and we may expect to see personnel departments eventually accepted throughout industry, whether it be in factories where goods are manufactured or in hospitals where bodies and souls are healed. The personnel worker has the opportunity of the pastor to minister to individuals without the burden of a budget or a ladies aid society.

Among physicians there exists a plan of consultation, wherein two or more physicians examine a patient and then, through discussion together, decide upon diagnosis and treatment. Likewise the clergyman may hold such consultation in behalf of a parishioner. This may be with a physician, a public health nurse, a personnel worker in industry, an attorney, or a social worker. As life in our modern society becomes increasingly complicated, the pastor cannot expect, nor need he feel obliged, to carry full responsibility for a parishioner whose life becomes tangled to the point of needing help. It must be remembered, however, that the individual decides whom he will select as his spiritual adviser. As professional people we may make elaborate plans, we may have highly skilled training, we may agree who shall do what and how, but the individual will make the final choice as to how he shall be helped, if and when he desires help.

The clergyman needs to recognize that there are others who

work in the spiritual area besides himself. He need not become apprehensive lest he lose his flock. If he is dealing with life realistically and helpfully, he will have work to do; if he is not, then the sooner he passes from the scene the better.

We often see an attitude of possessiveness among professional people toward their patients, clients, parishioners. It is *my* patient, *my* client, *my* parishioner, and resentment is expressed toward anyone else entering into the emotional picture. This is a sign of emotional immaturity and insecurity on the part of the worker. Far better is the attitude I heard expressed recently by a pastor who said, "I care not where they go so long as they receive what they need."

A. The Clergyman and Physician

Formerly the doctor and minister were contained in the same person, in the tribal medicine man; as such he gave more attention to the care of the soul than he did to the body. Trouble in the body meant that there was trouble in the soul.

As the healing art began to be practised separately from organized religion it is not surprising that the church fought its development. The old always struggles against the new, for the new is a threat to the existence of the old. An interesting example of the struggle between religion and medicine took place in England. When anaesthesia first began to be used to relieve the pain of childbirth the English clergy protested, claiming that such a practice was against the laws of God. Woman had sinned in the Garden of Eden and God had cursed her through the pain of child-bearing; if it had been meant to be otherwise, they said, childbirth would have been free from pain. This controversy continued until an English physician pointed out that in the Genesis story of creation God Himself had used anaesthesia in that He had caused Adam to fall into a "deep sleep" when Eve was created from the rib of Adam. After that the controversy quieted down.

More progress has been made in the last hundred years in the relief of physical pain than in all the rest of human history. Scientific medicine is less than a hundred years old. The doctor welcomed its advent with enthusiasm. "Now," he said, "I can treat disease. Now I can be free from that troublesome creature, the patient. All I want from him is that he pay his bill." So the doctor of the early twentieth century went about the practice of scientific medicine, only to find that if disease were treated without treating the patient, his bill was not paid and all too often the patient did not get well. Today the physician is recognizing that both disease and patient must be treated if good results are to be obtained.

The doctor holds as his task, "the alleviation of suffering and the prolongation of life." What the individual does with life when he has it the physician is not inclined to ask. He would be content, and often is, with the treating of symptoms, or the relief of physical pains. The conscientious physician, who conceives of his task in the broadest sense, who is motivated by a genuine affection for his fellow creatures, is not content with treating symptoms. He desires to see life lived happily and creatively because, in helping to achieve that condition, the joy of sound work comes to him; as a scientific man he has observed that disease is defeated where there is purposefulness in living. He gains little satisfaction in bringing about a cure of disease in a prostitute knowing that upon the recovery of her health she will return to her sordid trade; yet as a physician his work includes the sinner as it does the saint. As a practical human being, but not as a physician, he does ask, "What are you going to do with health when you have it?"

That is the question the clergyman asks also, only he speaks of *life* instead of *health*. Theoretically the clergyman is interested primarily in quality of living while the physician is interested in quantity of living. The clergyman, because he believes in a love of God that is not limited by time, does not care greatly when you die, except as your death affects your loved ones, for he believes that in death your life and work continue and he does not think of that as tragic. The physician's task is to keep you living as long and with as little suffering as possible; the clergyman's task is to help you live creatively and turn even your suffering and death into triumphant experiences.

In actual practice the physician and clergyman often are working upon the same specific problems. Because of the gap between our two professions which was increased with the coming of scientific medicine, and because of the lag in the training of clergymen for the practical task of ministering to individual persons, the doctor and minister have worked independently of each other to the patient-parishioner's detriment. I discovered a doctor and minister who were both trying to prevent a man from committing suicide. Each thought that he was the only one who knew of the man's trouble. United in the task through consultation together they presented a strong combination.

A significant factor which makes it difficult in some instances for the physician and clergyman to work together is that the two make their livings in different ways. The doctor is paid by the individual patient, the minister is paid by a group. I have never found it difficult to work with a successful doctor, nor with one who was really interested in his patient's welfare. These are men who feel economically and emotionally secure with their patients. The doctor who feels possessive is one who has but few patients. The exceptions to this observation are the doctors who have had a bad time with a clergyman in other cases, or who have a sense of guilt toward the church because of their own past experience with it. I know many physicians, who never go near churches, who are deeply religious men. They have a profound respect for nature and the dependability of nature. I have yet to talk with a sincere physician about his work that I did not feel I was talking with a religious man, even though he might not openly profess his faith.

Marked gains have been made in bridging the gap between the physician and clergyman; as we define our tasks more clearly and have a better understanding of each other's methods this gap will close more completely.

As clergymen we need to recognize that the physician is employed to assist a person to recover his health and is responsible for the patient during that time. He may be discharged by the patient or the family but he is responsible so long as he is employed. Therefore, if the clergyman comes into the picture he does so only with the physician's consent. The relationship between our two professions has been such that as ministers we seldom are barred from the sickroom and we rarely bother to obtain the physician's specific consent to call upon his patient. Likewise, seldom does the physician request our assistance. Until we reach the time when our mutual tasks are more clearly understood we would do well to be certain that we do as little harm as possible in the sickroom, and we must remember that the physician is employed to run the case and is responsible for doing so.

A telephone call to him, telling him you are Mrs. Blank's pastor and that you wonder how you can be most helpful to her will reassure the physician concerning your judgment. If there is some question in your mind about your ministry he will often have ideas as to how you can help. You may have known her for years while he will have known her a few days; even so, he will know her better than you do. Likewise, the clergyman needs to be cautious about advising a parishioner to go to a church hospital unless the local physician consents. I know a clergyman who has become very unpopular in his community with the physicians because he advises everyone to go to the hospital of his communion. A religion and health movement in which physicians and clergy were cooperating failed in an eastern city some years ago because the clergymen would not cooperate with physicians in the community who were not active in the movement.

Ideally, the physician, *not the clergyman,* as Dr. Richard Cabot said in our book, *The Art of Ministering to the Sick,* is the general. The doctor will decide what is needed for a patient even though he will not suggest specifically how the clergyman shall proceed with his task. That is, the doctor will think of the minister as working to strengthen a patient's morale, which may effect a recovery; he will not decide whether the clergyman's method should be listening, prayer, or communion. Just as he turns to the surgeon for a particular type of work, so he will turn to the clergyman.

In Chicago a woman was brought into the hospital by her minister because her local physician had told the minister he was unable to help her further. The local pastor asked me to see her so that I knew her from the time of her admission. She gave a history of prolonged abdominal pain, also a past history of five or six operations, the reasons for which appeared questionable to our physicians. They were questionable in that they were the kind a persistent patient could trick a surgeon into performing. Even though our physicians doubted that the woman had organic disease they decided to do a complete physical examination. To their surprise the X-ray examination revealed a small tumor of the lower bowel. They felt it improbable that this tumor should have caused her abdominal distress but decided to operate. Surgery of this nature is a psychologically mutilating procedure in that the diseased segment of bowel is removed and an artificial anus is made through the wall of the abdomen so that defecation takes place through the patient's side. From the standpoint of psychic shock this is one of the most serious surgical procedures done and yet hundreds of them are performed every year and the patients respond quite satisfactorily.

The operation was performed upon our patient and the surgeon was delighted at what he was able to accomplish. The tumor proved to be cancer but it was in its early stages. Convalescence is slow in these cases but in this one it was particularly slow; the patient just would not fight. Finally she was sent home, only to return later with many complaints, among which was one concerning her heart.

I had been seeing her regularly, and had had prayer several times with her. She was responsive but I always left with a feeling of discouragement. After her return to the hospital the internist (general physician), the surgeon and I got together for a consultation. We decided upon psychic shock treatment. She was to be told by the surgeon that she had had a cancer (she had always been afraid of cancer), that the cancer had been removed, that she could live six months or ten years, but that if she continued as she was she would not only kill herself but her husband also. My role was to swing her mind away from herself and build up her morale in any way that I could. As yet it is too soon to know how well we succeeded but we feel we did not get far. We were hampered because our treatment was too superficial. What she needs is a complete psychoanalysis to enable her to understand herself and her attitudes and that is not available.

In Boston a patient asked to see a minister before her operation and the request came to me. Following her operation, which was unsuccessful, I called upon her frequently, so that as she approached death her attitude was such that the tragedy of the experience was removed for the girl as well as for her family. A few months later the surgeon who had operated upon this girl had a similar case in another girl who was about the same age. The doctor, remembering the first, suggested to the family that she come into my care. Despite the fact that the family was active in a church which was some distance away, so that her own minister could not see her, they refused to agree with the surgeon's request for me to see her. That being the case we could do nothing further. The surgeon had turned to the minister because he recognized the problem and because he had seen favorable results in another case where the situation was the same.

In other instances I have been asked by attending physicians to see patients who are apprehensive. Many times I have been requested to see patients who have become discouraged because they are lonely and who face a long convalescence. In fact that group make up the major number of our requests from physicians. Where we see a person at the physician's request we go with an added authority. In the hospital where I now serve as chaplain I frequently make rounds with the physicians at their request. In this way I have an opportunity to become acquainted with patients who might want, and be aided by, spiritual counseling.

The physician and clergyman strengthen each other's work to the benefit of the patient when they work together; when they work independently of each other the patient is not best served. A physician friend of mine, Dr. Paul Ledbetter of Houston, Texas, has said repeatedly, "The cat is on the back of the clergy. When they are trained and prepared to handle these problems the doctor will gladly welcome them as coworkers." I think he is absolutely right. When the clergy comes to understand its task in the sickroom, as in the whole pastoral field, the physician will welcome him as a co-worker.

B. THE CLERGYMAN AND NURSE

It is not unusual for the nurse to know the patient better than the physician does. She is in and out of the patient's room many times a day, while the physician comes only for a few minutes. When the doctor enters the room the patient often responds to his interest and may appear better than he is; when the nurse comes in the patient relaxes into his true mood.

Some of my most important requests to see patients have come from nurses; this was true when I served as pastor of a church as well as in the hospital as chaplain. I made it a point to get to know as many nurses as possible. The nurse is a friendly person; she has to be or she fails as a nurse. Since she is trained to work with her hands, her mind works in a direct way. If she has seen the clergyman help one person she believes he might help another, so she calls him. It is that simple. If she sees a patient weeping she inquires why the tears and sets out to do something about them. Since she is a person of action she is apt to be aggressive in the spiritual area. If you encourage her to call you when your parishioner is discouraged she will do it and not know or care how busy you are. It is your job to help people and she will expect you to do it. If you inquire about a patient's condition she will tell you in so far as she is permitted. She cannot give you a diagnosis because that is against the rules, although she may in some instances. When calling in a hospital the clergyman should inquire of the nurse concerning the patient. If you stumble over a bed pan going in to see a parishioner neither your patient's spiritual condition nor your own will be helped by your call. The nurse can help you avoid such an error. If there is a "No Visitor" sign upon the door of your parishioner's room be certain to speak to the nurse, and introduce yourself as the patient's clergyman. In most instances you will be admitted, except at those times when you should not be. If there is still some question in your mind, then call the physician. The nurse works under his direction and is not responsible for the orders he has given except in carrying them out.

The public health nurse is a different type of person from the institutional or private duty nurse. She is apt to know more about the social condition of a community, the cesspools of crime, and the hovels of poverty than any other person in the community, including social workers. If you are interested in how the other half lives your public health nurse will know; she will welcome your interest and will often turn to you for help in given problems if you encourage her to do so. She will also be able to help you by acting as mediator in those difficult cases requiring a subtle approach. The clergyman needs the nurse just as he needs the physician if his work is to be widespread and effective.

C. THE CLERGYMAN AND SOCIAL WORKER

It is more difficult to describe the clergyman's relationship to the social worker than to the physician because the social work field is more complicated. There are almost as many types of social work as there are religious organizations and they come into existence for about as much reason as new religious sects spring up. It is said in Boston that if you need social service care for a flea you will find some agency there for such care. The depression and now the war have increased this American tendency to form new organizations.

One cannot speak authoritatively in describing the social work field but in general there are the public or tax supported agencies and the privately supported agencies. The tax supported agencies work in the field of relief, rehabilitation, child care, health and care of the aged; the private agencies work in the field of limited relief, rehabilitation, child care, family welfare, health, and care of the aged. The private agencies are now coming to be supported by community chests through voluntary contributions. They pioneer fields of social need and can set standards more readily than can the tax supported agencies. We expect to see a dropping off of private and an increase of tax supported agencies in the future, just as we have seen the church slowly moving out of such social work as the giving of relief, child care and the maintenance of homes for the aged.

We see the social worker, under the term of case-worker, doing pastoral work but calling it something else. The clergyman has not known whether to welcome her as a co-worker or to oppose her as an intruder; actually we find him doing both but unable to understand why he does either. The case-worker has been at a loss to understand the clergyman's attitude toward her because she has forgotten she is doing a type of work which the clergyman has carried single-handed for centuries. The clergyman has watched social work developing for some years, many ministers have gone into the field of social work themselves and have become leaders there; some have returned to the ministry, for in social work they missed the comfort of the altar. Now we are recognizing that the case-worker has definitely entered the pastoral work field even though she speaks a different vocabulary and her purpose is often different from ours.

When she talks about adequate food, clothing, and shelter for her clients we understand her and join forces with her in trying to coerce indifferent politicians into fulfilling their obligations even though few of her clients may be actually our parishioners. When she takes over the task of caring for orphans and placing them in desirable homes we rejoice and gladly send her families that are anxious to adopt babies. When she is able to counsel with problem parents about problem children we welcome her help; if she would only do something with our neurotic women as we send them to her we would ordain her into full membership in the ministry.

The social worker is content with treating symptoms, as the doctor often is; she talks of "adjustment" which means lack of conflict or suffering. She discovers the clergyman working to establish conflict and blames him for all the pathological guilt feelings she sees in her people. She does not recognize that the clergyman is as anxious to relieve such guilt as she is and often can do it more effectively, for he has *a different authority*. In time the case-worker will discover, as the physician is just beginning to discover, that the "adjusted" person, like the "healthy" person, is one who has reached a reconciliation between himself and his universe; he is one who has come to an understanding of God and has learned how to live creatively in a world which at its heart is creative.

For my part, I welcome the social worker into the pastoral work field; there is more than enough work for all. Our great need is not for fewer workers but for better cooperation between those that we have, as well as for constantly more able workers, but that is the need in every field. Fifty per cent of our population has no active church affiliation, and half of those who do belong to a church are not in touch with it, while a significant group of the remaining twenty-five per cent do not have a clergyman that can help them in case of need or they are unwilling to turn to him, for a variety of reasons. As an estimate, the church is serving spiritually perhaps fifteen per cent of our people. What about the rest? Where will they find spiritual advisers? Social case-workers, like physicians, will serve some of them. The others will limp along as sick people do, lost spiritually, and emotionally unhappy, social cancers in the body politic.

Some years ago in Chicago we desired to study this problem of cooperation between the clergyman and the social worker; we decided to do it upon the basis of what had already been done in individual cases. We requested the leading case-work agencies to submit records for the study. In all the records of the agencies we found but one instance where the clergyman had been active in cooperating with a case-worker and that was a bizarre case of a prostitute who kept trying to commit suicide; we were inclined to think such a case was unusual in the average clergyman's work, so that our study was not fruitful except in showing us how little cooperation there was.

As a pastor I turned to social workers for the following assistance:

1. Help in securing positions, particularly for psychoneurotic men who had returned from military service, where interpretation was needed with the prospective employer; with a man who had been in prison and who was having difficulty securing work; with a widow whose father was a difficult problem;

2. Persons needing financial relief;

3. Couples who were seeking babies for adoption;

4. Persons needing old age assistance;

5. Persons needing hospitalization who could not pay;

6. Persons who needed the public health nurse;

7. Persons who needed practical nurses;

8. For help in getting a patient admitted to a mental hospital;

9. For help with a handicapped child who needed to be placed in a home for the handicapped;

10. For help in making a plan and securing care for an expectant unmarried mother;

11. For help with a young woman who was having marital difficulty with whom I was too closely tied emotionally to be able to see her problem objectively;

12. For help with a girl who was having trouble with her father and who was blocked emotionally so that she could not talk with a man about her attitude toward men due to her fear of her father. The girl needed to talk to a woman.

Only in the two latter instances did I withdraw from the situation.

Social workers have sought my assistance with the following problems:

1. Ministry to the seriously ill and dying;

2. Consultations to decide if a person soon to die should be told he is facing death;

3. Persons facing long convalescence;

4. For help in securing funds for burial of a person who had died;

5. For help with bereaved persons;

6. For help in securing medical treatment for a child where no public funds were available;

7. Persons needing marital counseling;

8. For help with aged persons who had few callers;

9. To perform the marriage ceremony for an unmarried pregnant girl and her fiancé;

10. For help in taking a patient to a mental hospital;

11. When the husband of a patient died suddenly I was asked to tell her;

12. For help in talking to a boy about going to school who had spent all his life with women and who disliked women.

The clergyman is seldom thought of as being a resource person by the social worker, just as the clergyman often overlooks social resources which the social worker will have or know about.

When I was lecturing for the Y. M. C. A.—U. S. O. I found some communities where social workers and clergy had never sat down together to discuss their mutual problems. In Memphis, Tennessee, there is a regular monthly meeting where social workers and clergy meet together. It is amazing how many problems, methods and ideals we have in common when we get together and examine them.

I used to tell my theological students, "When you go to a community get to know your social workers." One wrote back after a few months and said, "You told us to get to know our social workers. I did when I came to this town. I have just married one that I met here." That is one way of getting acquainted across the professional lines, but it seems like carrying the matter of cooperation a little far if the two groups are to keep their individual identity.

CHAPTER XVII

THE NEW EVANGELISM

As HAS been said elsewhere, fifty per cent of the total population have no active church affiliation of any kind; fifty per cent of those who have an affiliation are inactive, while half of the remaining twenty-five per cent make little significant contribution to the life and program of the church. It is safe to say that ninety per cent of our members are born into the church and take it pretty much for granted until some crisis arises in their lives; then they either do not know how to tap the resources of religion, or the church in its ministry fails to reach them for a number of reasons.

The first task of evangelism is with those already within the membership of the church. This is a two-fold task: first, it is an educational responsibility. One of the most damning charges against organized religion that has come from our men in the combat theatres of the war is, "You did not teach us how to pray." You do not have to go to the war to observe this fact; go to a hospital, stand beside the bereaved, talk with the aged, inquire of new members why they have sought membership in the church and you find how limited most people are in their understanding of religion. One wonders, what have we been teaching in the church anyway? It is so easy to go off into ethereal realms to escape the hard task of interpreting life as it is lived, so easy to withdraw behind cloistered walls and dream. The hard question we ought to be asking our religious leaders and those who occupy our pulpits and the seats of the learned, is simply, "Does what you are teaching and preaching

help with the job of living? Will it help a man to die who wants
to live? Will it help a woman to live whose heart has died? Does
it have toughness in its fiber, and courage at its core? Will it
touch selfishness; is it greater than hate?"

The kind of religion we need is portrayed in an autobio-
graphical book entitled *Convert to Freedom*.[1] Eitel Wolf
Dobert, a former German Nazi, tells the story of a French
officer, named Bach, who was, at the time Dobert knew him,
working to improve relations between France and Germany.
"Bach had served seventeen years as an officer in the French
army. He went through the entire war of 1914–18, having
been wounded three times. After the Armistice he reached
the Rhine with his battalion, burning with hatred. During
the occupation of the Ruhr region he was entrusted with the
command of Datteln and came into violent conflict with the
mayor, a fanatical German patriot, who categorically declared
that he would obey no French command. Following the Easter
holidays the mayor was supposed to be arrested.

"On Good Friday Bach went to church. From his corner he
quietly listened to the sermon. After the service the minister
celebrated Communion. Slowly figures emerged from the dark
colonnades on either side and strode to the altar.

"Suddenly all were frozen into silence. The two arch enemies,
Bach and the mayor, stepped up to the altar at the same moment. One question could be read in all eyes. Would they both
drink from the same cup?

"The cup trembled in the minister's hand. Above it loomed
the cross!

"But the two men had only one thought. If enmity was to
transcend the all-pervading love of the sacrament—then away
with a religion which had picked the idea of Christianity down

[1] G. P. Putnam's Sons, p. 200. New York, 1940.

to the bare bones of a few empty formulas. In the little church the people, as though hypnotized, watched the two kneeling men receive Communion from the same cup.

"From that moment on Bach was convinced that there was something above patriotism. His relations with the German authorities immediately improved. The arrest of the mayor was not carried out."

The clergy, going into the Navy, have attended a chaplain's training school at Williamsburg, Virginia. When I was visiting there in June, 1943, I sat in a class where the candidates were preaching before Chaplain C. H. Lambdin, then dean of the school. They were supposed to be delivering sermons they would preach in a few weeks when they received their assignments with the Navy. Some of the sermons were little more than a string of pious phrases lifted from religious literature. Finally Chaplain Lambdin, who had recently returned from two years of duty aboard a transport, interrupted a candidate who was particularly poor. "Wait a minute," he said, "I'm a gob from Brooklyn. I've never been inside a church before. You've got ten minutes to catch my interest. Do you think you can do it with that pious stuff?" It is something like that that we must ask our ministers and teachers of religion.

The second task of evangelism lies in the area of pastoral work. Until we can do the job as I have outlined it in these pages we have no right to go to the fifty per cent of our population that is unchurched with the message of our Lord, for we are hypocrites when we talk about the love of God in Christ but are unwilling and unable to demonstrate it to those who have already sought that love in the fellowship of the church. We hear cries go up that the church is not holding its membership. Of course it isn't. Will a barrenness of spirit, constant pleas for money, and a terrific sense of guilt within the worshiper, which goes unalleviated, hold people whose souls cry out for comfort and whose spirits seek courage and a challenge?

The pastor may well say, "Very well, how do you propose to accomplish this tremendous task of evangelism of the church's own membership through education and pastoral work? There is only so much time and one pastor can serve only a limited number of people."

A pastor friend of mine said recently, "The next church I take I am going to use sermons out of the barrel and ring door bells for the first year." If he rings door bells, walks hospital halls, and ferrets out his members in their places of residence and work for a year, his sermons will have a ring of authority and affection that will overflow his "barrel" to become a spring of living water. Let the minister, upon coming to a new assignment, first seek out the acutely ill, the dying, and the recently bereaved. Then he should call upon the members of his official board, the officers of his women's society, his young people's society, and his church school teachers; then he may go to the shut-ins and aged. After that, still keeping up his calls upon the sick regularly, he may start his routine calling, upon every family, day after day and week after week, the regular in atendance, the indifferent and indolent. Let him be certain that new plans and new organizations are withheld until those door bells have been rung and every person called upon. Watch the life of that church begin to stir!

There is a strong tendency among people, seeking a church home, to affiliate with the big church. (By "big" I mean a church with over eight hundred members.) Nothing succeeds like success; people are attracted to the church whose program is active and where large crowds congregate. While there are many strengths in a "big" church, such as beauty of architecture, good music, interesting preaching, still there are distinct limitations in a "big" church, also. People become lost in the crowd and frequently miss a feeling of fellowship; they come to think of the church as indifferent and cold, and gradually drop out of active membership. The tragedy of the "big" church is that so many people come in the front door but are lost through indifference. The Roman Catholics seem to be able to handle large churches; for them a membership of four, six and even eight thousand souls is not unusual in the large cities. Such a parish is under the care of a pastor, who is assisted by a sufficient number of priests to carry on the work.

Few of our Protestant clergy seem to be able to work with assistants because they are unable to delegate work. Also, people are unwilling often to accept the ministry of assistants. Our pastors sometimes refuse the suggestion of an official board that assistants be employed to help with the church's program, while other boards see no need for such assistants. There is a trend toward employing women as church callers to assist in the pastoral work of the church. In many instances a pastor who cannot work with another minister works well with a woman assistant. This plan holds merit but we have done little toward training such callers and, until we do, the program faces definite limitations. Our large churches are manned by men with preaching ability, most of whom have little interest in pastoral work. So long as this situation continues to be true the large church will continue to fail its people. Failure in churches with large memberships is not so obvious as in a small congregation because of the numbers of people who come to the church every Sunday. The pastor of a Baptist church of five thousand members in a southern city found he was reaching twelve per cent of his membership, yet his sanctuary was filled every Sunday, his church school program was strong, his women's society active and money for the budget came easily. He had been so impressed by the "visitors" who came and went that he did not realize that his own membership had largely given up attending the church.

In the Church of Scotland it was customary formerly for the elders to call upon each family every quarter to pass out communion tokens. On Communion Sunday parishioners were not admitted to the "kirk" unless they presented a token. In this way each elder came to have spiritual care of a given number of persons. In time of illness or misfortune, the elder was called; he in turn might call the pastor. The result was that pastors could come and go, but the life of the church remained unbroken because the spiritual care of the parish continued. This practice has fallen into disuse due to the tendency in Scotland, as in the United States, to make religion more and more the "business" of the minister and less and less the concern of the layman who is content with paying the bills. When I asked a Presbyterian elder who had grown up under the old Scotch system what he thought of the plan for American churches he replied, "I doubt if there are many members of the official boards of our American churches who would be up to it spiritually." Perhaps if we inaugurated such a program they would become inspired to deepen their spiritual lives so that they would be "up to it." Too often we have been content to let the official board run the financial affairs of the church while the pastor did the rest. If a significant program of evangelism through pastoral work and education is carried on the layman will have to do something besides "pay and sit," and most people are quite willing to do so when given leadership.

I believe a number of laymen could be found in every large church who have natural talents and with pastoral encouragement could develop an interest in doing calling under the minister's direction. The Methodist Church has raised up and put to effective use "the lay preacher." It also has the "lay leader." Why would it not be possible to develop "lay pastoral workers" and give them definite status in the church and before the congregations?

The evangelistic preaching of another generation has passed, except in a few sections of the country. Yet there is need for a program of intensive work in each congregation at least once a year. A congregation needs to hear a new voice, to come into contact with another personality than the one they hear week after week.

A plan being experimented with in several churches is an adaptation of one long used by the Episcopalians, that is the holding of a week of worship and preaching services, called *missions,* for which a "visiting" clergyman is brought in to carry on the preaching. His sermons are of an inspiration and instruction type, as contrasted to those that seek to reach the unchurched person. They are directed toward the church member. In addition to the formal services appointments for personal counseling are emphasized. These appointments may be held at the clergyman's hotel or in the church office, or at both places.

When I was conducting seminars upon *Religion and Health* for Jesse Bader's National Christian Missions, a number of people always sought appointments to talk about personal difficulties. When I would inquire, "Have you talked with your pastor about this?" they would usually answer, "Oh, I wouldn't want him to know about it." The point was that I was leaving town next week and the parishioner would not see me again. Further, I had not known the parishioner in the past, therefore would not be shocked by the story. We ought to give our parishioners an opportunity to make their confessions and secure help through personal counseling with another clergyman if they prefer. In practice many of our parishioners seek a certain kind of assistance from another minister anyway while parishioners of another church come to us.

In closing may we examine the high calling of the pastor as he goes about his work. In the following ~~~~~~~~~ ~~~~~~on, which is an adaptation of one I once wrote concerning the pastor's ministry to the sick, the parishioner speaks.

The Pastor

Today a pastor came to see me. I didn't know much about him before he came, nor did he know much about me. I didn't know much about him after he had left for I seem to have done most of the talking. Well, maybe I was the one who needed to talk for things don't seem to have been going very well. I don't just know why but they haven't.

He sat down and we talked. He inquired how I liked the weather and when I told him, "Not much" he smiled and said he didn't either. Curious how many things can be said about the weather with a person you don't know very well, while you're sort of sizing each other up. What you say isn't important but it kind of gives you time to get the feel of each other. Like feeling the solid flesh of a fine horse you're looking over. After you've had a hand on a horse your eyes tell you more of what you're seeing than before. The weather is a convenient subject to talk about when you are starting a conversation.

He asked me about my work. Presently I found myself talking about it. I told him how long I'd been on my present job and how I did it. As I talked I found myself interested in things I always had taken for granted. He didn't say much, just asked a few questions but there was a twinkle in his eye that showed he was interested. As we talked I thought of ways of doing my work a little better than I'd ever done it before. Guess it's not such a bad job after all. Curious how some one encouraging us to talk about our job whets our keenness for it.

He asked about my family. I was surprised that he knew a lot about that boy of mine. Seems like they've had some talks together and that the boy has grown up. Here I didn't even know he's been thinking about going to school so's to get some special training. I didn't tell the pastor about some of the trouble the boy's had because it's all past now but I'll bet he could have helped me if I had when I needed someone to talk to. I didn't tell him about a lot of things I've wanted to talk to someone about, but he's the kind of person who would have listened and not stopped me before I could get started.

After he left I felt like doing something hard, something I would have to stretch to do. Funny I should feel that way just because a minister talked to me a little while. After he had gone I wanted to whistle. Things seem to be going pretty good now and they're going to go better. The old world is a pretty good place after all.

That pastor is awfully familiar, come to think about it. No stranger about him. I've heard something about someone being sick and someone going to call, about being in prison and someone's going there. Suppose I've been in prison? Kind of locked up in my own problems and here a stranger unlocks the door?

> A stranger came to Jerusalem
> And stood on the temple steps,
> They dragged him through the city streets
> To a cross above the city
> *That's where I have seen him before*
> *On a cross above the city.*"

The pastor's task is to personalize *the man on the cross*.

APPENDIX

BIBLIOGRAPHY OF PASTORAL AID BOOKS

These books may be used by the pastor as aids in his work by placing them in the hands of the parishioner.

On Wings of Healing, edited by John W. Doberstien. $2.00. Muhlenberg Press, Philadelphia, 1941. For the sick.

A Diary of Private Prayer, Baillie. $1.50. Charles Scribner's Sons, New York, 1936. A collection of beautiful prayers, arranged for morning and evening private devotions.

The Meaning of Prayer, Fosdick. $1.00. Association Press, New York. The classic upon prayer.

The Temple, Orchard. $.75. E. P. Dutton & Company, Inc. New York, 1920. A book of prayers.

Lift Up Your Hearts. Bowie. $1.00. The Macmillan Company, New York, 1939. Meditations, prayers and litanies.

Abundant Living, Jones. $1.00. Abingdon-Cokesbury Press, Nashville, 1941. Daily readings, meditations and prayers with particular attention to the relation between religion and health.

Five Minutes a Day, Speer. $1.00. Westminster Press, Philadelphia, 1943. Meditations, poetry and inspirational readings.

The Glory of God, Harkness. $1.00. Abingdon-Cokesbury Press, Nashville, 1943. Prayers and poems of an inspirational and devotional nature.

Living Every Day, Newton. $2.25. Harper and Brothers, New York, 1937. General readings of an inspirational nature, in short easy form.

The Stuff of Life, ibid. $2.00.

Living Up to Life, ibid. $2.25.

You Must Relax, Jacobson. $1.75. Whittlesey House, New York, 1942. Deals with the art of physical relaxation.

My Companion for Quiet Hours, Bahnsen. 24 for $1.00. Church World Press, Cleveland, Ohio, 1941. A pamphlet, twenty-four pages. Meditations and prayers for the sick.

Quiet Corner, Strong. $.50. E. P. Dutton & Co., Inc., New York. Inspirational meditations and brief essays.

House of Dreams, ibid.

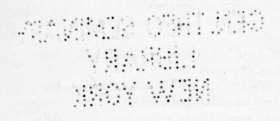